Books writt
Trust Go
What W
Never
How to Study the Bible
Quiet Confidence in the Lord
One Hundred Years from Today
Nuggets of Faith

Books co-authored with Judy Hartman

God's Plan for Your Life
You Can Hear the Voice of God
God's Instructions for Growing Older
Effective Prayer
Overcoming Fear
A Close and Intimate Relationship with God
God's Joy Regardless of Circumstances
Victory Over Adversity
What Does God Say?
Receive Healing from the Lord
Unshakable Faith in Almighty God
Exchange Your Worries for God's Perfect Peace
God's Wisdom Is Available to You
Increased Energy and Vitality

Scripture Meditation Cards
co-authored by Jack and Judy Hartman

Receive Healing from the Lord
Freedom from Worry and Fear
Enjoy God's Wonderful Peace
God Is Always with You
Continually Increasing Faith in God
Receive God's Blessings in Adversity
Financial Instructions from God
Find God's Will for Your Life
A Closer Relationship with the Lord
Our Father's Wonderful Love

God's Plan for Your Life

Jack and Judy Hartman

Lamplight Ministries, Inc., Dunedin, Florida

We are pleased that you have chosen to read this book. We trust that the Bible verses in this book and our explanation of this Scripture will help you find, enter into and successfully complete God's plan for your life.

We would like to hear from you. Please send us an email at lamplightmin@yahoo.com or drop us a note at Lamplight Ministries, Inc., P.O. Box 1307, Dunedin FL 34697. Please visit our website at www.lamplight.net and tell us about your adventure or call 1-800-540-1597 and leave a message for Judy.

You also can request our free newsletter by mail or email. We would be so pleased to stay in touch with you with our newsletter. You can see updates on forthcoming books and keep us in prayer as we pray for you. You also can receive a daily devotional from a set of our Scripture meditation cards. You can download the first chapter of each of our books.

We are blessed that you will get to know us through the pages of this book. We will look forward to hearing from you. We look forward to getting to know you.

Jack and Judy

ISBN: 978-0-915445-27-1

Library of Congress Control Number: 2013939539

Dedication

We dedicate this book to Dr. Kenneth and Dr. Deborah Friendly, pastors of Lighthouse Christian Fellowship, in Anchorage, Alaska. We are deeply honored that our publications fit so well into your vision for your church family: to help people understand the Word of God so that it is totally applicable to every area of their lives: spiritually, emotionally, financially, and physically. (See their website at lighthousealaska.org)

We thank you for building families solidly on the Word of God. We are so blessed that God has connected us to work together for His glory and our joy. We thank God that the light of Christ Jesus is shining vibrantly through you both and that hungry hearts in Alaska and across the globe are being ignited with a hunger for God and His message to them, His Word. Hallelujah! We love you.

Jack and Judy

Table of Contents

Introduction

The Bible teaches that God has a specific plan for the life of each person He has created. We will study Scripture that will show you that God has a plan for *your life*.

Many Christians go through life giving little or no thought to God's plan for their lives. Many of these Christians attend church regularly. They pray daily. They live a moral life. Living this way is excellent, but God has more for you. We ask you to approach this book with an open mind to see exactly what the Bible says about God's plan for your life.

I (Jack) wrote a book titled *God's Will for Our Lives* more than 25 years ago. I wrote this book when a Christian publishing firm approached me about writing books with them. I was flattered by this request. I wrote two books with this firm.

However, I was not able to do anywhere near the extensive scriptural research that we do on the books that we write today. We normally write six drafts of each book. Because the publisher of the previous book had a deadline, we were only able to do two drafts of *God's Will for Our Lives.*

This book was good as far as it went, but it did not go far enough. We have allowed this book to go out of print. We have titled this new book *God's Plan for Your Life* so that there will not be any confusion about duplication of titles.

Also, we want to explain that we have a set of Scripture Meditation Cards and an accompanying CD titled *Find God's Will for Your Life.* We believe that any Christian who sincerely desires to find God's assignment for his or her life will find many answers from the Bible in this book as well as in the Scripture cards and the CD. Please see the order form at the back of this book for ordering information.

We now use *The Amplified Bible* almost exclusively in our books. I (Jack) have been using *The Amplified Bible* since 1975. At that time only *The Amplified New Testament* was available. I bought this version of the Bible when I saw it in a Christian bookstore with an inscription from Dr. Billy Graham on the cover saying, "This is the best Study Testament on the market. It is a magnificent translation. I use it constantly."

The Amplified Bible is the result of the study of a group of Bible scholars who spent a total of more than 20,000 hours amplifying the Bible. They believe that traditional word-by-word translation often fails to reveal the shades of meaning that are part of the original Greek, Hebrew and Aramaic biblical texts.

Any amplification of the original text uses brackets for words that clarify the meaning and parentheses for words that contain additional phrases included in the original language. Through this amplification the reader will gain a better understanding of what Hebrew and Greek listeners instinctively understood.

We would like to give you an example of why we use *The Amplified Bible* almost exclusively:

- "I can do all things through Christ which strengtheneth me." (Philippians 4:13, *The King James Version*)
- "I can do all this through him who gives me strength." (Philippians 4:13, *The New International Version*)

- "I have strength for all things in Christ Who empowers me [I am ready for anything and equal to anything through Him Who infuses inner strength into me; I am self-sufficient in Christ's sufficiency]." (Philippians 4:13, *The Amplified Bible*)

Please note the significant amplification of the original Greek in *The Amplified Bible*. If you desire to meditate on Philippians 4:13, you will find that there is much more depth of meaning in *The Amplified Bible*. All Scripture references in this book are from *The Amplified Bible*.

As you read this book, we recommend that you highlight or underline all passages of Scripture that are meaningful to you and our explanation if it is helpful to you. Write notes in the margin or at the top or bottom of the page. If you do, you then will be able to go back through this book after you have read it the first time. You will be able to meditate on these meaningful passages of Scripture that you already have identified (see Joshua 1:8 and Psalm 1:2-3).

I (Jack) want to explain why I use the first person on many occasions in our books. I write the first two drafts of each book. Judy then adds her valuable input to the next two drafts. I then write the final two drafts.

I do not want to use the words "I (Jack)" every time I use a first-person reference. I will just use the word "I" when I make a personal observation during the remainder of this book. Any personal observations from Judy will be clearly identified.

Every principle that we will explain in this book is solidly anchored on Scripture. We explain each passage of Scripture in simple and easy-to-understand language. We pray that the scriptural contents of this book and our explanation of this Scripture will help you to find and carry out God's plan for *your* life.

Chapter 1

God Has a Specific Plan for Your Life

We will devote this book primarily to Scripture pertaining to God's specific plan for your life. Before we begin, we want to share important instructions that God gives to all of His children.

First and foremost, God's plan is for every Christian to ① love Him with his or her entire being, heart, soul, mind and strength (see Deuteronomy 6:5, Mark 12:30 and Luke 10:27). After you obey this instruction, you will be empowered to ② complete God's second instruction to love your neighbor as you love yourself.

Jesus Christ instructed us to be disciples (see Matthew 28:18-20 and Mark 16:15-18). These instructions must be woven into the tapestry of every life. You can only share your faith if you have a relationship with God through His Son, Jesus Christ.

The greatest sin in the church today is the sin of silence. If you are not sharing your faith in Jesus Christ with others, you are not growing in Him. Our prayer is that our writings will help your relationship with God to grow deeper every day so that your life will be so filled with the fullness of God that your faith bursts forth to others each day (see Colossians 2:9 and Ephesians 3:19).

Now that we have briefly summarized God's instructions to all of His children, we will devote the remainder of this chapter to Scripture explaining that God had a specific plan for your life before He created you in your mother's womb. There are approximately seven billion people living in the world at this time. Each person has different fingerprints. Each person has a unique DNA. The one exception is that identical twins sometimes have the same DNA.

There is no question that God has created every person, with the exception of identical twins, to be completely different. God's specific assignment for your life is just as individual as your fingerprints or your DNA.

God is omniscient. He knows every minute detail about every one of the more than seven billion people on earth. The psalmist David understood this great spiritual truth. He said, "O Lord, you have searched me [thoroughly] and have known me. You know my downsitting and my uprising; You understand my thought afar off. You sift and search out my path and my lying down, and You are acquainted with all my ways. For there is not a word in my tongue [still unuttered], but, behold, O Lord, You know it altogether." (Psalm 139:1-4)

God knows every time that you sit down and every time that you stand up. He understands every thought that goes through your mind. He knows when you go to sleep at night and when you wake up. He knows every word that you speak. He even knows what you are about to say before you speak.

The same Almighty God Who created every planet, star and galaxy in the universe knows *you* intimately. He is very interested in you. You are special to Him. He took infinite care in creating you.

God decided who your parents would be, whether you would be male or female and where you would be born. He chose the color of your skin, your eyes and your hair. He determined who your brothers and sisters would be or whether you would be an only child.

God knew you intimately before He formed you in your mother's womb. The psalmist David knew that God had a specific plan for every day of his life. David said, "Your eyes saw my unformed substance, and in Your book all the days [of my life] were written before ever they took shape, when as yet there was none of them." (Psalm 139:16)

Even before God formed David in his mother's womb, every day of David's life already was planned. God knew exactly what He wanted David to do with his life. God made a similar statement pertaining to the life of the prophet Jeremiah. God said, "Before I formed you in the womb I knew [and] approved of you [as My chosen instrument], and before you were born I separated and set you apart, consecrating you; [and] I appointed you as a prophet to the nations." (Jeremiah 1:5)

Please note the similarity between what the Bible says about the lives of the psalmist David and the prophet Jeremiah. Both of these verses explain that God had a specific plan for each man's life before He created him in his mother's womb. The amplification in Jeremiah 1:5 says that Jeremiah was God's chosen instrument. God knew that Jeremiah would be a prophet to the nations before he was born.

If God had a specific plan for the lives of David and Jeremiah before they were born, you can be certain that God had a specific plan for your life before He created you. "...God shows no partiality and is no respecter of persons" (Acts 10:34)

We have explained that omniscient God knows every minute detail about the life of every person in the world. God knows you so well that He even knows every hair on your head. Jesus Christ said, "…even the very hairs of your head are all numbered." (Matthew 10:30)

Omniscient God is capable of knowing exactly how many hairs are on the head of every one of the billions of people on earth. He is capable of having an individual plan for your life and for the life of every other person He has created.

The following passage of Scripture describes the gifts that are given to people who receive Jesus Christ as their Savior. "Having gifts (faculties, talents, qualities) that differ according to the grace given us, let us use them: [He whose gift is] prophecy, [let him prophesy] according to the proportion of his faith; [he whose gift is] practical service, let him give himself to serving; he who teaches, to his teaching; he who exhorts (encourages), to his exhortation; he who contributes, let him do it in simplicity and liberality; he who gives aid and superintends, with zeal and singleness of mind; he who does acts of mercy, with genuine cheerfulness and joyful eagerness." (Romans 12:6-8)

Most Christians have one primary gift and one or more secondary gifts. Your special gift from God is given to you to enable you to carry out God's assignment for your life.

Read the list of talents in this passage of Scripture. Do any of these talents describe you? If so, you may begin to see what God wants you to do with your life. If you are not sure what talents you have and what God wants you to do with your life, study these gifts. Pray continually asking God to reveal every detail about His plan for your life.

Romans 12:6 instructs you to *use* the gifts and talents that God has given to you. Do not allow these talents to lie dormant. As you learn your specific God-given talents and you work at developing these talents, you will be doing what God created you to do. As you study the Scripture in this initial chapter, we pray that you will be highly motivated to seek, find and carry out the specific assignment that God has for your life and to develop and use the talents and abilities He has given to you.

If Jesus Christ is your Savior, you have been given the ability to learn exactly what God created you to do. "…we are God's [own] handiwork (His workmanship), recreated in Christ Jesus, [born anew] that we may do those good works which God predestined (planned beforehand) for us [taking paths which He prepared ahead of time], that we should walk in them [living the good life which He prearranged and made ready for us to live]." (Ephesians 2:10)

If you do not understand what we refer to when we speak of receiving Jesus Christ as your Savior, please stop now and go to the Appendix at the end of this book. Your entire life will be transformed when and if you receive Jesus as your Savior. Please contact us so that we can celebrate your being born again into God's family.

Ephesians 2:10 says that you are "recreated in Christ Jesus [born anew]." When you receive Jesus Christ as your Savior, you are born again. You were born physically when you emerged from your mother's womb. You experience a definite and specific spiritual rebirth when Jesus Christ becomes your Savior (see John 3:3-7).

Ephesians 2:10 tells you that God had a specific plan for your life that He prepared in advance. God wants you to walk in this plan – to successfully complete the assignment He has given to you and to use the specific talents and abilities that He has given to you.

You cannot do the good works that God created you to do until Jesus Christ becomes your Savior. When Jesus becomes your Savior, Satan's demons no longer will be able to prevent you from learning God's will for your life. You will "…escape out of the snare of the devil, having been held captive by him, [henceforth] to do His [God's] will." (II Timothy 2:26)

Satan and his demons do not want you to seek, find and carry out God's assignment for your life. Satan wants you to waste your life by devoting your life to the pursuit of personal goals. Satan's demons do their best to deceive every person from finding out and carrying out God's assignment for his or her life. "Many plans are in a man's mind, but it is the Lord's purpose for him that will stand." (Proverbs 19:21)

Many people have their own plans for their lives. Turn *away* from self-centered goals to do what God created you to do. Only God's purpose will stand the test of eternity.

Chapter 2

The Eternal Significance of God's Assignment for Your Life

God gives each person complete freedom of choice. You can make the choice to focus on seeking, finding and carrying out God's will for your life or you can do whatever you want to do during the remainder of your life. The apostle Paul said, "Everything is permissible (allowable and lawful) for me; but not all things are helpful (good for me to do, expedient and profitable when considered with other things). Everything is lawful for me, but I will not become the slave of anything or be brought under its power." (I Corinthians 6:12)

Paul explained that you are free to do whatever you want to do, but many choices that Christians make are not expedient and profitable. Paul stated that he would not be the slave of anything. He would not allow selfish desires to dominate his life. Do not make the mistake of using the freedom of choice that God has given you to devote the remainder of your life to the pursuit of personal goals. "...be careful that this power of choice (this permission and liberty to do as you please) which is yours, does not [somehow] become a hindrance..." (I Corinthians 8:9)

Pray each day asking God to guide you to do what He wants you to do. Constantly turn away from the world to draw closer to God so that you can hear His voice. "…in Christ Jesus, you who once were [so] far away, through (by, in) the blood of Christ have been brought near." (Ephesians 2:13)

If you have received Jesus Christ as your Savior, you no longer are far away from God. The shed blood of Jesus Christ has enabled you to have a close and intimate personal relationship with God. "The secret [of the sweet, satisfying companionship] of the Lord have they who fear (revere and worship) Him…" (Psalm 25:14)

This verse explains the secret of a close and intimate relationship with God. You will be close to God to the degree that you fear Him, revere Him and worship Him. Fear of God is reverent awe for Him. If you truly fear God, He will be at the center of your life. If you have reverent awe for God, you will be highly motivated to seek, find and carry out His assignment for your life.

A close and intimate relationship with God is very important for you to successfully complete His assignment for your life. If God is at the center of your life instead of your life revolving around your personal desires, you will be much more likely to find what God has called you to do with your life. Jesus said, "…Your will be done [held holy and revered] on earth as it is in heaven." (Luke 11:2)

These words are part of we call the Lord's Prayer. Jesus emphasized that every person on earth should do God's will just as every person in heaven does God's will. The words "holy and revered" in the amplification of this verse explain the priority that God places on seeking, finding and carrying out His will for your life.

God is holy. Everyone in heaven reveres Him. No one in heaven is proud. Everyone in heaven is humble and loving. No person in heaven pursues ungodly goals. Everyone in heaven does the will of God.

Do not focus your life primarily on the pursuit of personal goals. Revere God Who is holy. After reading the Scripture that we have studied so far in this book, make the quality decision to constantly seek God's will for your life. "…do not be vague and thoughtless and foolish, but understanding and firmly grasping what the will of the Lord is." (Ephesians 5:17)

People who devote their lives to pursuing personal goals are "vague and thoughtless and foolish." Be precise instead of being vague. Commit your life to seeking what God has called you to do and to successfully completing this assignment. "…the world passes away and disappears, and with it the forbidden cravings (the passionate desires, the lust) of it; but he who does the will of God and carries out His purposes in his life abides (remains) forever." (I John 2:17)

The Bible teaches that this world we live in ultimately will pass away (see Matthew 24:35). The craving that people have to pursue selfish desires will pass away. However, if you devote your life to seeking, finding and carrying out God's assignment for your life, your life will have eternal significance.

I am 81 years old as I write this book. My life is completely dedicated to carrying out God's assignment for my life. This is the 27th Christian book I have written (or co-authored with Judy). I know that God has called me to write these books. I am inspired by the outpouring of comments we have received from people in more than 60 countries who have been helped by our books and Scripture cards. I believe that God is calling me to write at least ten more books during the remainder of my life. I know that many people will be helped by these books after I have gone to be with the Lord.

I am experiencing great peace from knowing that I am doing exactly what God has called me to do. I pray that you will have a deep commitment to seek God's will for your life. "...learn to sense what is vital, and approve and prize what is excellent and of real value..." (Philippians 1:10)

As you grow and mature as a Christian, you will turn away from devoting your life primarily to the pursuit of selfish goals. You will look at life more and more from God's perspective. You will understand what is "vital, excellent and of real value." You will devote your life to doing God's will if you understand the eternal significance of successfully completing the assignment that God has given to you. You will be filled with God's joy.

Every Christian ultimately will appear before the judgment seat of Christ. What you have done during your life on earth will be judged at that time. "...we must all appear and be revealed as we are before the judgment seat of Christ, so that each one may receive [his pay] according to what he has done in the body, whether good or evil [considering what his purpose and motive have been, and what he has achieved, been busy with, and given himself and his attention to accomplishing]." (II Corinthians 5:10)

Please note the word "all" in this verse. You will appear before the judgment seat of Christ. You will be rewarded at that time for what you have done during your life. The amplification of this verse says that you will be judged based on the purpose and motive of your life on earth and what you have been busy with and given your attention to accomplishing.

If you make the quality decision to seek, find and carry out God's assignment for your life, you will be rewarded in heaven. You may not be a famous person on earth, but you will be honored in heaven. Jesus said, "…many who [now] are first will be last [then], and many who [now] are last will be first [then]." (Matthew 19:30)

Many people who are recognized on earth for their worldly accomplishments will not receive high honors in heaven. Many Christians who do not seem to have accomplished much from a worldly perspective will be honored in heaven for successfully completing God's assignment for their lives. "If then you have been raised with Christ [to a new life, thus sharing His resurrection from the dead], aim at and seek the [rich, eternal treasures] that are above, where Christ is, seated at the right hand of God." (Colossians 3:1)

Is Jesus Christ your Savior? If He is, you have been raised to a new life. Seek the eternal treasures that God has for you.

In Matthew 25 Jesus used a parable to explain what people on earth should do with the talents and ability that God gives to each of His children. In this parable Jesus explained the reaction of a man when he observed what one of his servants did with the talents and ability he had been given. He said, "…Well done, you upright (honorable, admirable) and faithful servant!" (Matthew 25:21)

This man was very pleased to see that his servant had devoted himself to using his talents to doing what he had called him to do. Do you have a deep desire to hear the words "Well done, good and faithful servant" spoken when you appear at the judgment seat of Christ? God instructs you to live "…as servants (slaves) of Christ, doing the will of God heartily and with your whole soul; rendering service readily with goodwill, as to the Lord and not to men, knowing that for whatever good anyone does, he will receive his reward from the Lord..." (Ephesians 6:6-8)

You are instructed to be a servant of Christ. The amplification uses the word "slave." God instructs you to do His will "heartily and with your whole soul." You will be rewarded for your commitment to God's will for your life.

If you are not rewarded at the judgment seat of Christ for successfully completing God's assignment on earth, you still will live throughout eternity in the glory of heaven. However, God will bestow glorious eternal blessings on His children who consistently turn away from the pursuit of personal goals to seek, find and carry out His assignment for their lives.

Chapter 3

The Total Commitment of Jesus Christ

In Chapter 1 we studied Scripture to show you that God has a specific plan for the life of each person He creates. In Chapter 2 we studied the eternal significance of seeking, finding and carrying out God's assignment for your life. In this chapter we will study what the Bible teaches about Jesus Christ and His commitment throughout His earthly ministry to successfully complete the assignment His Father had given to Him.

Jesus lived the only perfect life that has ever been lived. He came to earth as the Son of Man even though He was and is the Son of God. Jesus came to earth as a human being Who faced the same temptation to sin that every other human being faces.

Jesus is equal to God (see Philippians 2:6), yet He came to earth as a *servant*. Jesus said, "…whoever wishes to be great among you must be your servant, and whoever desires to be first among you must be your slave—just as the Son of Man came not to be waited on but to serve, and to give His life as a ransom for many [the price paid to set them free]." (Matthew 20:26-28)

These words that Jesus spoke to His disciples apply to your life today. If you have a sincere desire to be great from God's perspective, you can accomplish this goal to the degree that you live your life as a servant. Jesus used the word "slave" to describe how He lived during His earthly ministry. A slave is a human being who is owned by another human being. Jesus dedicated every aspect of His life to doing exactly what God had called Him to do.

Jesus chose to give up His equality with God. He did not choose His Deity during His earthly ministry. He lived throughout this time in relation to His Father just as you and I are given the privilege to do.

Jesus explained the deep hunger that He had to successfully carry out God's will for His life. "...the disciples urged Him saying, Rabbi, eat something. But He assured them, I have food (nourishment) to eat of which you know nothing and have no idea. So the disciples said one to another, Has someone brought Him something to eat? Jesus said to them, My food (nourishment) is to do the will (pleasure) of Him Who sent Me and to accomplish and completely finish His work." (John 4:31-34)

Jesus received spiritual nourishment from successfully completing God's assignment for His life. He said, "...I do not seek or consult My own will [I have no desire to do what is pleasing to Myself, My own aim, My own purpose] but only the will and pleasure of the Father Who sent Me." (John 5:30)

The amplification of this verse explains that Jesus had no desire to pursue personal goals. He was completely focused on doing what God sent Him to earth to do. Jesus said, "I receive not glory from men [I crave no human honor, I look for no mortal fame]" (John 5:41)

Some people are highly motivated to seek recognition from other people. Jesus Christ had no desire to receive recognition from other human beings. He repeatedly emphasized that His sole purpose was to do what God sent Him to earth to do. Jesus said, "...I have come down from heaven not to do My own will and purpose but to do the will and purpose of Him Who sent Me." (John 6:38)

God always emphasizes through repetition. Jesus said essentially the same thing in John 6:38 that He said in John 5:30. Do you have a similar commitment in your life?

One of the best examples of the commitment that Jesus had occurred in the Garden of Gethsemane. Jesus knew that Judas Iscariot would betray Him there and that He would be captured by soldiers (see Mark 14:41-43). He knew that He then would be sent to a whipping post to be horribly mutilated. He knew that He then would die a horrendous death on the cross where He actually would become sin as He took the sins of every person upon Himself.

Once again we want to emphasize that Jesus came to earth as the Son of Man – a human being just like you. "...Jesus went with them to a place called Gethsemane, and He told His disciples, Sit down here while I go over yonder and pray. And taking with Him Peter and the two sons of Zebedee, He began to show grief and distress of mind and was deeply depressed." (Matthew 26:36-37)

Please note that this verse says that Jesus "began to show grief and distress of mind and was deeply depressed." Jesus Christ, Who is equal to God, experienced great agony at Gethsemane. "Then He said to them, My soul is very sad and deeply grieved, so that I am almost dying of sorrow. Stay here and keep awake and keep watch with Me." (Matthew 26:38)

Jesus was so grieved that He was almost dead because of His great sorrow. "And going a little farther, He threw Himself upon the ground on His face and prayed saying, My Father, if it is possible, let this cup pass away from Me; nevertheless, not what I will [not what I desire], but as You will and desire." (Matthew 26:39)

Crucifixion was such a severe method of punishment that Roman citizens could not be crucified. Only the very worst criminals from other countries could be crucified. Jesus knew that He faced a punishment that was so excruciating that Roman citizens could not be crucified.

Jesus reacted the same way that you probably would react if you knew you were about to go through the grievous ordeal that He faced. In His humanity, Jesus threw Himself on the ground. He prayed asking God if there was any way He could avoid having to pay the price that He knew He was about to pay. In His agony Jesus then said the words that are *vitally* important to each of us. Even though He had just asked His Father if He could escape this horrible ordeal, Jesus said that He did not want to do what He desired, but what God had called Him to do. Jesus paid an *enormous price* to carry out His Father's will.

A tremendous spiritual battle was fought that night at Gethsemane. Jesus turned away from the agony that He was about to suffer to express His total commitment to carrying out God's will for His life. Just before He was about to be betrayed by Judas and turned over to a group of soldiers (see John 18:2-12), Jesus was determined to give glory to God. He said, "I have glorified You down here on the earth by completing the work that You gave Me to do." (John 17:4)

Jesus gave glory to God by completing the work that God gave Him to do. You will glorify God to the degree that you turn away from personal goals to successfully complete the assignment that God has for you.

The gospels of Matthew, Mark, Luke and John explain the agony that Jesus went through after Judas and the soldiers captured Him. In the final agonizing moments before He died, Jesus said three of the greatest words that have ever been spoken. "…He said, It is finished! And He bowed His head and gave up His spirit." (John 19:30)

When Jesus said "It is finished," He referred to completing the assignment that God had given to Him to take all of the sins of the world upon Himself. None of us will ever have an assignment from God that even approaches the difficulty of the assignment that Jesus was given. As you study and meditate on the Scripture in this chapter and throughout this book, we pray that you will become totally committed to seeking, finding and successfully completing the assignment that God has given to you.

Chapter 4

Your Life Belongs to Jesus Christ

You have learned that God has a specific plan for your life and that you will be rewarded in heaven if you seek, find and successfully complete God's assignment for your life. We have studied the life of Jesus Christ during His earthly ministry. You have seen that Jesus was totally, completely and absolutely committed to carrying out God's assignment for His life.

Jesus paid an enormous price so that all of your sins are forgiven and that you will be able to live with Him throughout eternity in the glory of heaven. Because Jesus paid this price for you, your life belongs to Him. "...You are not your own, you were bought with a price [purchased with a preciousness and paid for, made His own]. So then, honor God and bring glory to Him in your body." (I Corinthians 6:19-20)

This verse explains that your life does *not* belong to you. If Jesus Christ is your Savior, your life belongs to Him because of the awesome price He paid for you. You are instructed to honor God and to bring glory to Him by the way you live.

Many people today want to do what they want to do when they want to do it. Many years ago a popular song was titled "I Did It My Way." As you grow and mature as a Christian, you will find that true meaning, satisfaction and fulfillment will only come to you to the degree that you turn away from all selfish goals and desires. If you had a song about your life, that song should be titled "I Did It Your Way, God."

We will study Scripture in a subsequent chapter explaining that Jesus Christ is omnipresent just as God is omnipresent. In addition to sitting on a throne next to God in heaven, Jesus also lives in the heart of every Christian. If Jesus is your Savior, He lives in *your* heart. His desire is for you to surrender control of your life to Him (see Galatians 2:20).

Jesus fully understands God's plan for your life. If you willingly surrender control of your life to Him and allow Him to live through you, you will find, enter into and successfully carry out God's assignment for your life. The quality of your life will be much better than if you were in control.

God's plan is for Jesus Christ to be much more than your Savior. God's plan is for Jesus to be Lord of every day of your life. Many people are on the throne of their lives. They are their own little gods. Get off the throne. Put Jesus there where He belongs. Allow Him to guide you into the center of God's plan for your life. "...the love of Christ controls and urges and impels us, because we are of the opinion and conviction that [if] One died for all, then all died; and He died for all, so that all those who live might live no longer to and for themselves, but to and for Him Who died and was raised again for their sake." (II Corinthians 5:14-15)

The love of Christ is the key to the life of every person. Please note that the word "all" is used four times in this passage of Scripture. God is emphasizing that He is speaking to every person on earth. The word "all" includes you. Jesus Christ died for you so that you will "live no longer to and for yourself." Jesus wants you to live for Him because He "died and was raised again for your sake."

Why would you want to control your life if you are certain that the victorious Jesus Christ Who rose from the dead lives in your heart? He will control your life to the degree that you surrender control to Him. Jesus died so that your life will be much more meaningful and fulfilling than if you are constantly pursuing personal goals.

You will only complete God's assignment for your life to the degree that Jesus Christ truly is in control of your life. As you grow and mature spiritually, you will become increasingly motivated to totally surrender control of your life to Him. The apostle Paul said, "None of us lives to himself [but to the Lord], and none of us dies to himself [but to the Lord, for] if we live, we live to the Lord, and if we die, we die to the Lord. So then, whether we live or we die, we belong to the Lord." (Romans 14:7-8)

Please note the word "none" at the beginning of this passage of Scripture. No person should live for himself or herself. The Word of God instructs each of us to dedicate our lives to the Lord. Your life belongs to Jesus Christ. Gladly allow Him to take His rightful place. Center your life around your commitment to yield control to Him.

Jesus is much better equipped to control your life than you are. He said, "...If anyone intends to come after Me, let him deny himself [forget, ignore, disown, and lose sight of himself and his own interests] and take up his cross, and [joining Me as a disciple and siding with My party] follow with Me [continually, cleaving steadfastly to Me]." (Mark 8:34)

The word "anyone" in this verse includes you. Jesus instructs you to deny yourself. The amplification of this verse says that you should "forget, ignore, disown and lose sight of yourself and your own interests." You can only find and successfully complete God's assignment for your life to the degree that you willingly surrender control of your life to Jesus Christ.

Jesus instructs you to take up your cross. When He refers to taking up your cross, He speaks of dying to personal goals just as He died for you. The amplification of this verse instructs you to follow Jesus continually. You are instructed to "cleave steadfastly" to Jesus. The word "cleave" in this context means to adhere to, to cling to and to be faithful. The word "steadfastly" means unchanging and unwavering. Cling to Jesus continually. Allow Him to live in you and through you.

The most important decision that you will ever make is to receive Jesus Christ as your Savior. The next most important decision is to willingly and gladly surrender control of every day of your life to Him. "...those who belong to Christ Jesus (the Messiah) have crucified the flesh (the godless human nature) with its passions and appetites and desires." (Galatians 5:24)

If your life truly does belong to Jesus Christ, you will *crucify* your God-given right to control your own life. The amplification of Galatians 5:24 speaks of "the godless human nature." Every person, with the exception of Jesus Christ Who was born of a virgin and therefore was not a direct descendant of Adam, inherited the godless nature of Adam. "...all seek [to advance] their own interests, not those of Jesus Christ (the Messiah)." (Philippians 2:21)

Every person, except Jesus Christ, was born with an inherent desire to be selfish. Selfishness comes naturally to us.

Selflessness does not come naturally to us. The quality of your life will improve significantly as you learn to die to your selfish desires and willingly surrender control of your life to Christ Jesus. Jesus said, "…whoever loses his [lower] life on My account will find it [the higher life]." (Matthew 10:39)

The word "whoever" in this verse applies to you. You will only find the higher level of God's will for your life to the degree that you willingly commit to turn away from the lower life of consistently pursuing personal desires.

You can identify people who have surrendered their hearts to Jesus Christ. You would classify them as "givers." Some people are naturally helpful as part of their personality. These people more easily give their lives to Jesus Christ. When you meet people, you often can sense whether they are givers or takers. You will notice a special joy in the lives of givers. They have given their lives to the Lord. Their lives are not their own. They live in relation to Him.

God has a much better life planned for you than you can possibly understand with the limitations of human logic and comprehension. Give up control of your life to Jesus Christ Who gave His life for you.

God's ways are much higher than the ways of human beings (see Isaiah 55:8-9). Most people think that they will be free if they are doing what they want to do with their lives. Just the opposite is true. True freedom comes from surrender. You will be free in the spiritual realm to the degree that you willingly surrender control to Jesus Christ to dedicate your life to doing what God created you to do.

Jesus Christ loves you so much that He was beaten, whipped, crucified and became sin for *you*. If you comprehend the enormity of the sacrifice that Jesus made for you, you will gladly surrender control of your life to Him.

Make the quality decision to commit every day of your life to Jesus Christ just as He made the supreme commitment that enables you to live throughout eternity with Him in the glory of heaven. The remainder of your life on earth is a *very* short time compared to what is the equivalent of trillions of years of eternity. Do not waste precious time pursuing personal goals. Be determined to seek, find and carry out God's assignment for your life. The quality of every day of your life will be much better than if you were in control.

Chapter 5

Deterrents to Completing God's Assignment for Your Life

Now that you have seen what the Bible says about your life belonging to Jesus Christ, we are ready to look into God's Word to learn what it says about some of the things that stop Christians from carrying out God's assignment for their lives. Here in the United States preoccupation with money and the possessions that money can buy often is a significant deterrent to completing God's assignment. Some Christians spend large amounts of time and energy attempting to accumulate wealth. "Let your character or moral disposition be free from love of money [including greed, avarice, lust, and craving for earthly possessions] and be satisfied with your present [circumstances and with what you have]" (Hebrews 13:5)

Please note the words "character or moral disposition" in this verse. If you obey God's instructions to renew your mind by studying His Word each day (see II Corinthians 4:16 and Romans 4:23) and to meditate day and night on His Word (see Joshua 1:8 and Psalm 1:2-3), your character will be much more in conformity to God's instructions than if you do not do this daily Bible study and Scripture meditation.

We live in a materialistic society. The words "craving for earthly possessions" in the amplification of Hebrews 13:25 describe the attitude of many people in the world today. Our society places so much emphasis on homes, cars, clothing and other things that money can buy that many people are focused on accumulating wealth. Jesus Christ said, "No one can serve two masters; for either he will hate the one and love the other, or he will stand by and be devoted to the one and despise and be against the other. You cannot serve God and mammon (deceitful riches, money, possessions, or whatever is trusted in)." (Matthew 6:24)

You decide whether preoccupation with wealth or a consistent focus on serving God will be the dominating factor in your life. Jesus said that you cannot serve God and also pursue wealth. The words "deceitful riches" in the amplification of this verse are an accurate description of what happens to many people who pursue wealth. Some people believe that everything will be great if they had a large amount of money. If they are successful in accumulating this money, they often find that their lives are empty and meaningless. Wealth does not provide deep meaning and fulfillment.

The Bible teaches that you should work diligently to earn an income to support your family (see I Timothy 5:8). Expend the energy to support your family, but do not fall into the trap of pursuing excessive wealth over and above your needs and the needs of your family. "…the love of money is a root of all evils; it is through this craving that some have been led astray and have wandered from the faith and pierced themselves through with many acute [mental] pangs." (I Timothy 6:10)

This verse explains the problems that people bring into their lives when they love money. You cannot love money and love God at the same time. The Bible teaches that you should place your love for God ahead of your love for anyone or anything else (see Matthew 22:37-38).

Many readers of this book know wealthy people who live empty lives. The love of money can cause you to wander from your faith in God and bring problems into your life. This verse says that the love of money is "a root of all evils." Satan and his demons use the love of money to deceive many people to live in a way that is not in obedience to God's instructions in the Bible. If you read and obey the scriptural instructions in this book, we believe that you will place the desire to seek, find and carry out God's assignment for your life ahead of the pursuit of wealth or anything else.

Another deterrent to carrying out God's assignment for your life is attempting to understand life through the limitations of worldly logic and understanding. If you pay the price of getting into God's Word every day and getting God's Word into you, you will program yourself to think the way that God thinks, not as the world thinks. "Lean on, trust in, and be confident in the Lord with all your heart and mind and do not rely on your own insight or understanding. In all your ways know, recognize, and acknowledge Him, and He will direct and make straight and plain your paths." (Proverbs 3:5-6)

God says that you should not rely on the limitations of human insight and understanding. If you program your mind with God's Word each day and you put Him in first place and keep Him there, He will "direct and make straight and plain your paths." "Man's steps are ordered by the Lord. How then can a man understand his way?" (Proverbs 20:24)

God wants you to allow Him to direct your steps. You cannot carry out God's assignment for your life with the limitations of human logic and understanding. "There is a way which seems right to a man and appears straight before him, but at the end of it is the way of death." (Proverbs 14:12)

If you do what seems right to you based on the limitations of human understanding, you will be spiritually dead. You will be dormant in the spiritual realm. You cannot understand God's ways, including His plan for your life, by doing what seems right to you. We often say that God emphasizes through repetition. Please note what God says in a subsequent verse of Scripture. "There is a way that seems right to a man and appears straight before him, but at the end of it is the way of death." (Proverbs 16:25)

Instead of always doing what seems right to you, God instructs you to program your mind each day with His Word (see II Corinthians 4:16). God instructs you to yield control of your life to the Holy Spirit so that He can direct your steps. "...the mind of the flesh [which is sense and reason without the Holy Spirit] is death [death that comprises all the miseries arising from sin, both here and hereafter]. But the mind of the [Holy] Spirit is life and [soul] peace [both now and forever]." (Romans 8:6)

Once again you are told that you will be dead spiritually if you attempt to live by the limitations of human sense, logic and reason instead of yielding control of your life to the Holy Spirit. You are spiritually dormant when you are in control of your life. You are spiritually alive to the degree that the Holy Spirit is in control of your life.

Your loving Father assures you that He will give you the wisdom and understanding that you need to carry out His will for your life. "The reverent fear and worship of the Lord is the beginning of Wisdom and skill [the preceding and the first essential, the prerequisite and the alphabet]; a good understanding, wisdom, and meaning have all those who do [the will of the Lord]. Their praise of Him endures forever." (Psalm 111:10)

If you fear God, you revere Him and hold Him in constant awe. Your life revolves around your certainty of His indwelling presence. You will receive God's wisdom when you truly fear Him.

Please note the word "all" in this verse. Every person who is carrying out God's will for his or her life will receive good understanding, wisdom and meaning from God. God promises to give you supernatural wisdom whenever you need His wisdom. "If any of you is deficient in wisdom, let him ask of the giving God [Who gives] to everyone liberally and ungrudgingly, without reproaching or faultfinding, and it will be given him. Only it must be in faith that he asks with no wavering (no hesitating, no doubting). For the one who wavers (hesitates, doubts) is like the billowing surge out at sea that is blown hither and thither and tossed by the wind. For truly, let not such a person imagine that he will receive anything [he asks for] from the Lord, [for being as he is] a man of two minds (hesitating, dubious, irresolute), [he is] unstable and unreliable and uncertain about everything [he thinks, feels, decides]." (James 1:5-8)

Please note the word "any" at the beginning of this passage of Scripture. If any Christian lacks wisdom to carry out God's will or for any other reason, this person is instructed to ask God. If you have absolute faith that God will give you the supernatural wisdom that He promises to give you, you will receive His wisdom. However, if you allow doubt and unbelief to discourage you from doing what God has called you to do, you will block God. You will be double-minded. Your mind will go back and forth from fear to faith.

Your Father wants you to be single-minded. He wants you to be absolutely certain that He will provide everything you need to successfully complete His assignment for your life. "…He lavished upon us in every kind of wisdom and understanding (practical insight and prudence), making known to us the mystery (secret) of His will (of His plan, of His purpose)…" (Ephesians 1:8-9)

The word "lavished" means extravagant and abundant. God will give you more than enough wisdom to do everything He has called you to do to successfully complete His assignment for your life. If you run into obstacles as you pursue His plan, meditate on the Scripture we are studying here. Know that your loving Father will give you all of the wisdom you need to find and carry out His assignment for your life.

In this chapter we have studied what the Word of God says about the pursuit of wealth and the limitations of human logic, intellect and understanding blocking you from carrying out God's will. In the next chapter we will look further into the Word of God for additional information that will explain how some Christians are blocked from completing God's assignment for their lives.

Chapter 6

Turn Away from the World

Some Christians block themselves from carrying out God's plan for their lives because of their preoccupation with worldly activities. The Bible says that Jesus Christ has set you free from the ways of the world. "...our Lord Jesus Christ (the Messiah), Who gave (yielded) Himself up [to atone] for our sins [and to save and sanctify us], in order to rescue and deliver us from this present wicked age and world order, in accordance with the will and purpose and plan of our God and Father" (Galatians 1:3-4)

Jesus Christ, Who paid the price for the sins of every person, also paid the price to rescue and deliver you from the wickedness that pervades the world. Turn away from the ways of the world if you truly desire to carry out God's plan for your life. If Jesus Christ is your Savior, this world is not your home. The Bible speaks of Christians as being "...aliens and strangers and exiles [in this world]..." (I Peter 2:11)

You may be listed in worldly records as a citizen of a specific country, but the truth is that all Christians actually are citizens of heaven. You are just passing through this world for a relatively short period of time before you go on to live throughout eternity in your real home in heaven. "...we are citizens of the state (commonwealth, homeland) which is in heaven…" (Philippians 3:20)

If Jesus Christ is your Savior, you are a foreigner and an alien in the world. The more that you grow and mature as a Christian, the more you will turn away from the ways of the world. Jesus was crucified on the cross at Calvary to pay the price to crucify the world to you and you to the world. The apostle Paul spoke of "…our Lord Jesus Christ (the Messiah) through Whom the world has been crucified to me, and I to the world!" (Galatians 6:14)

Please note that the same word "crucified" that is used to describe the death of Jesus Christ on the cross is used in regard to your relationship to the world. God wants you to *die* to the ways of the world. He does not want you to allow anything in the world to significantly influence your life. Jesus has paid the price to set you completely free from the influence of the world to pursue God's will for your life.

The more that you grow and mature as a Christian and live the way the Word of God instructs you to live, the more some unbelievers will look at you with disdain. Jesus said, "If the world hates you, know that it hated Me before it hated you. If you belonged to the world, the world would treat you with affection and would love you as its own. But because you are not of the world [no longer one with it], but I have chosen (selected) you out of the world, the world hates (detests) you." (John 15:18-19)

If your commitment to Christ causes some people to oppose you, you are in good company. Many people were strongly opposed to Jesus during His earthly ministry. These people hated Jesus because His ways were very different from their ways. If you grow and mature as a Christian and turn away from the world, some people will strongly oppose you because your beliefs are so different from what they believe.

These people have no alternative from their perspective. If what you believe is right, this conclusion would mean that what they believe is wrong. They will not accept this premise. "Do not love or cherish the world or the things that are in the world. If anyone loves the world, love for the Father is not in him. For all that is in the world—the lust of the flesh [craving for sensual gratification] and the lust of the eyes [greedy longings of the mind] and the pride of life [assurance in one's own resources or in the stability of earthly things]—these do not come from the Father but are from the world [itself]." (I John 2:15-16)

The Word of God emphatically instructs you not to love the world or things in the world. You cannot love the world and love God. The ways of the world and God's ways are very different (once again, see Isaiah 55:8-9).

As you come more and more into God's will for your life, you will find that many things that used to be important to you no longer have significance and meaning to you. As you grow and mature as a Christian, you will consistently learn and obey God's instructions. You show your love for God by consistently learning and obeying His instructions (see John 14:24 and I John 2:5 and 5:3).

The ways of the world are externally oriented. As you grow and mature as a Christian, you will live more and more from the inside out, not from the outside in. The Bible teaches that God, Jesus Christ and the Holy Spirit make their home in your heart (see I Corinthians 3:16, II Corinthians 13:5, Ephesians 3:17 and 4:6 and Colossians 2:10).

As you become more internally oriented and live your life based on the indwelling presence of God, you will turn away from external things in the world. The amplification in I John 2:16 speaks of "the pride of life [assurance in one's own resources or in the stability of earthly things]." As you grow and mature, you will turn away from trusting in yourself. You will place all of your trust in God. Your security will not come from worldly sources. Your security will come from God.

There is a direct ratio between your maturity as a Christian, completing God's assignment for your life and turning away from the ways of the world. "…Do you not know that being the world's friend is being God's enemy? So whoever chooses to be a friend of the world takes his stand as an enemy of God." (James 4:4)

You cannot be a friend of the world and carry out God's plan for your life. The more that you are caught up with people, places, things and events in the world, the more you will turn against God and His supernatural plan for your life. Be like the psalmist who prayed to God saying, "Open my eyes, that I may behold wondrous things out of Your law. I am a stranger and a temporary resident on the earth; hide not Your commandments from me." (Psalm 119:18-19)

If you consistently fill your eyes, your ears, your mind, your heart and your mouth with the Word of God, you will learn supernatural Truth from God. You will understand that you are a only a temporary resident in the world. You will not be caught up with the ways of the world if you program yourself continually with the Word of God.

I often think about things in the world that used to be important to me that no longer are important. I am not talking about things that are evil. One example that I can give is the preoccupation that I had with following sports when I was younger.

I still follow sports, but nowhere near to the degree that I used to. I used to know all the batting averages of the baseball players. I used to scour the fine print of the sports pages in our daily newspaper to learn every detail about the sports

I followed. The word "fan" in "sports fan" means fanatic. Some people are fanatical about sports. Their lives revolve around sports.

You may have had other worldly interests in your life than sporting events. You may have been interested in activities that are not evil in themselves. We are not saying that everything in the world is evil, although many things in the world are much more evil today than when your parents and grandparents were your age. We are saying that you can only find, enter into and successfully complete God's assignment for your life to the degree that you turn *away* from allowing yourself to be significantly influenced by anything in the world.

We now will study what the Bible says about the influence of Satan in your life and the relationship between his influence and completing God's plan for your life. The Barna Research Group surveys the beliefs of Christians and unbelievers. One of their surveys showed that 47% of the Christians they surveyed believe that Satan is only an evil symbol, not a living entity.

Dr. George Barna, the founder of the Barna Research Group, said, "Hollywood has made evil accessible and tame, making Satan and his demons less worrisome than the Bible suggests they are. It is hard for achievement-driven, self-reliant, independent people to believe that their lives can be impacted by unseen forces."

The purpose of this chapter is not to give a full explanation of Satan and his demons and their ability to influence people. A Christian cannot be demon-possessed. If Jesus Christ is your Savior, He lives in your heart (see II Corinthians 13:5, Galatians 2:20 and Ephesians 3:17). There is no way that Satan can possess you if the victorious Jesus Christ lives in your heart.

However, Christians can be demon-oppressed. You can be oppressed by demons to the degree that you allow Satan's demons to oppress you. Satan deceived Eve in the Garden of Eden (see Genesis 3:1-6). Satan was able to influence Judas Iscariot to betray Jesus Christ (see John 13:2).

The Bible teaches that Satan and his demons are angelic beings. They are invisible. They can whisper into a person's ear. This person will think that the thought is coming from his or her own mind. You can tell if Satan is whispering in your ear if you have thoughts that are contrary to God's thoughts in the Bible.

Do not be like the Christians who were surveyed by the Barna Group who do not believe that Satan is who the Bible says he is. Jesus Christ once said, "…Get behind Me, Satan! For you do not have a mind intent on promoting what God wills, but what pleases men [you are not on God's side, but that of men]." (Mark 8:33)

This verse of Scripture refers to a statement that the apostle Peter made to Jesus after He spoke of His forthcoming death. Jesus knew that Peter's statement was influenced by Satan. Jesus replied to Satan, not to Peter. Please note that Jesus said that Satan is not intent on promoting what God wills.

Satan and his demons will do everything they can to deceive you from seeking, finding and successfully completing God's will for your life. Instead, Satan wants you to focus on things that please men – the things of this world. "We know [positively] that we are of God, and the whole world [around us] is under the power of the evil one." (I John 5:19)

The influence of Satan and his demons in the world has intensified greatly during the last 40 or 50 years. Most mature Christians believe that we live in the last days before the return of Jesus Christ. Satan and his demons are doing everything they can to influence as many people as they can to turn toward the ways of the world and to turn away from the ways of God, including the will of God for every person He created. "…be subject to God. Resist the devil [stand firm against him], and he will flee from you. Come close to God and He will come close to you.…" (James 4:7-8)

Submit to God. Study and meditate on God's Word every day. Learn God's instructions. Obey His instructions. Learn God's promises. Have absolute faith in the reliability of His promises (see Numbers 23:19, Joshua 23:14, I Corinthians 1:9, II Corinthians 1:20 and Hebrews 6:8). When you do these things, you are being subject to God. You then will be able to effectively resist Satan's attempts to deceive you from seeking, finding and carrying out God's will for your life. If you stand boldly against Satan based on the Word of God, Satan and his demons will flee.

Verse 8 says that, if you to come close to God, He will come close to you. You decide how close you will be to God. You decide how much you will allow Satan to influence your life. You are told that God will come close to you if you come close to Him. Make the quality decision to turn away from the ways of the world and from the influence of Satan and his demons to successfully complete God's assignment for your life.

The atmosphere around you is filled with Satan's demons and God's angels. You decide whether your words and actions will activate God's angels (see Psalm 103:20) or whether you will consistently allow Satan to deceive you.

Christians who are in the center of God's will for their lives are a significant threat to Satan. If you are pursuing God's will for your life, you can be certain that Satan and his demons will do anything they can to stop you. The remainder of this book is filled with specific instructions from your loving Father telling you exactly what to do to seek, find and carry out His plan for your life.

Chapter 7

The Word of God and the Will of God

You cannot find God's will for your life unless you obey His instructions to study and meditate each day on His Word. The Word of God is God's general will for all of His children. The more that you learn about God's general instructions for all Christians, the better foundation you will have to learn God's specific instructions for your life. Consistent study and meditation on the Scripture references in this book will help you to become increasingly sensitive to God's specific plan for your life.

Your mind can be compared to a computer. A computer will not produce effective results if it is not properly programmed. God instructs you to consistently program supernatural data from His Word into your mind to find His plan for your life. The more that you program the Scripture references in this book into your mind and your heart, the better equipped you will be to find and carry out God's assignment for your life.

If you renew your mind by studying the Word of God each day (see II Corinthians 4:16 and Ephesians 4:23), you will consistently program yourself with supernatural instructions and promises from God. "Do not be conformed to this world (this age), [fashioned after and adapted to its external, superficial customs], but be transformed (changed) by the [entire] renewal of your mind [by its new ideals and its new attitude], so that you may prove [for yourselves] what is the good and acceptable and perfect will of God, even the thing which is good and acceptable and perfect [in His sight for you]." (Romans 12:2)

The amplification in this verse explains that the world operates primarily through "external, superficial customs." Romans 12:2 explains that your life will be *transformed* if you consistently renew your mind in the holy Scriptures. The Greek word that is translated "transformed" in this verse is "metamorphoo." The English word "metamorphosis" that means a complete change comes from this Greek word.

Your life will be *completely changed* if you consistently renew your mind in the Word of God. Additional amplification in this verse explains that you will develop "new ideals and a new attitude" if you consistently renew your mind in God's Word. You then are told that renewing your mind in God's Word will prove God's perfect will for your life.

This powerful verse of Scripture is filled with information from God that will help you to find His perfect will for *your* life. "…this is how we may discern [daily, by experience] that we are coming to know Him [to perceive, recognize, understand, and become better acquainted with Him]: if we keep (bear in mind, observe, practice) His teachings (precepts, commandments)." (I John 2:3)

This verse of Scripture explains how to know God more intimately on a daily basis. There is no question that a close and intimate relationship with God is required to learn His plan for your life. This verse says that you will consistently become better acquainted with God if you learn and obey His instructions. You will be like the psalmist David who said, "I delight to do Your will, O my God; yes, Your law is within my heart." (Psalm 40:8)

If your heart is filled with the Word of God, you will delight in seeking, finding and carrying out God's will for your life. You cannot do anything that is more helpful to finding God's plan for your life than to fill your heart with God's Word as a result of daily Scripture meditation.

We now are ready to study the one verse of Scripture that we use in almost all of our books. "This Book of the Law shall not depart out of your mouth, but you shall meditate on it day and night, that you may observe and do according to all that is written in it. For then you shall make your way prosperous, and then you shall deal wisely and have good success." (Joshua 1:8)

This verse consists of specific instructions that God gave to Joshua when he succeeded Moses as the leader of Israel. When we study this magnificent verse of Scripture, we always study the last part first. If Joshua did what God instructed him to do at the beginning of this verse, God promised Joshua that he would be prosperous, that he would make wise decisions and that he would be successful. These same blessings apply to *your* life.

The word "prosperous" in this verse means much more than financial prosperity. The Hebrew word "tsalach" that is translated as "prosperous" here means to press forward, break out and go over. If you obey the instructions in Joshua 1:8, you will press forward, break through and go over obstacles that could prevent you from successfully accomplishing God's will for your life.

The Bible contains more than 500,000 words. *Strong's Exhaustive Concordance of the Bible* lists every word in the King James Bible. The word "success" is used *only one time* in the entire Bible – in Joshua 1:8. This verse explains exactly what to do if you truly desire to be successful in finding and carrying out God's specific plan for your life (or if you desire to be successful in any other area).

Now that we have studied what God promised to Joshua (and to you in regard to seeking God's will for your life), we are ready to study the first portion of this verse that tells you exactly what God instructs you to do to receive the blessings from Him that we have just studied. First, you are told that the Word of God should flow out of your mouth continually. You then are told that you should meditate day and night on the Word of God. If you meditate on the Word of God, you will speak God's Word continually.

The Hebrew word "hagah" that is translated as "meditate" in this verse means to "speak, talk, utter." You *will* speak God's Word constantly if you meditate on it day and night. As this process continues over a period of time, you will "observe and do" more and more of what God has instructed you to do. If you obey these three instructions from God, you will receive the blessings that God promises in the last half of Joshua 1:8.

We suggested in the Introduction that you highlight or underline all Scripture in this book that is meaningful to you. If you do this, you are *studying* the Word of God. If you highlight and underline as you read this book for the first time, you will identify specific Scripture to subsequently *meditate* on as you seek God's assignment for your life.

When you finish this book, we recommend that you go back to the Scripture that you originally highlighted or underlined. Meditate day and night on this Scripture. *Speak* these specific instructions and promises from God. If you continually speak these passages of Scripture and personalize them as you meditate on them, you will fill your heart with the Word of God. The Holy Spirit will use this Scripture in your heart to reveal more and more of God's specific plan for your life.

Chapter 8

God Is the Potter and You Are the Clay

In Chapters 5 and 6 we looked at different obstacles that cause some Christians to block themselves from carrying out God's assignment for their lives. In the last chapter we studied the relationship between daily Bible study and Scripture meditation and carrying out God's will for your life. We will begin this chapter by examining the relationship between what the Bible teaches about humility and God's will for your life.

There is a definite relationship between spiritual maturity and how humble you are. "Who is there among you who is wise and intelligent? Then let him by his noble living show forth his [good] works with the [unobtrusive] humility [which is the proper attribute] of true wisdom." (James 3:13)

Proud people are self-centered. Their lives revolve around themselves. They sit on the throne of their lives where God is meant to be. When this verse and the amplification instruct you to be humble so that you will show forth good works, these words include God's plan for your life.

You are doing good work when you are carrying out God's assignment for your life. This verse and the amplification instruct you to have "unobtrusive humility." The word "unobtrusive" means not to call attention to yourself.

If you are a mature Christian, you will consistently put God first, other people second and yourself last. "Do nothing from factional motives [through contentiousness, strife, selfishness, or for unworthy ends] or prompted by conceit and empty arrogance. Instead, in the true spirit of humility (lowliness of mind) let each regard the others as better than and superior to himself [thinking more highly of one another than you do of yourselves]." (Philippians 2:3)

You are instructed to do nothing that is based on pride, conceit or selfishness. God instructs you to have a "true spirit of humility" where you consistently look at other people as being more important than yourself. If you truly are humble, you will think more about other people than you do about yourself.

Even if you are highly educated, skilled and successful from a worldly perspective, God instructs you to put other people ahead of yourself. This attitude is essential to successfully carrying out God's assignment for your life. "Let each of you esteem and look upon and be concerned for not [merely] his own interests, but also each for the interests of others." (Philippians 2:4)

The words "each of you" in this verse include you. Your Father again instructs you to be concerned with the interests of other people, not just yourself. "Let this same attitude and purpose and [humble] mind be in you which was in Christ Jesus: [Let Him be your example in humility:] Who, although being essentially one with God and in the form of God [possessing the fullness of the attributes which make God God], did not think this equality with God was a thing to be eagerly grasped or retained, but stripped Himself [of all privileges and rightful dignity], so as to assume the guise of a servant (slave), in that He became like men and was born a human being." (Philippians 2:5-7)

The holy Scriptures instruct you to be humble just as Jesus was humble throughout His earthly ministry. This passage of Scripture speaks of Jesus being equal to God. Philippians 2:5 explains that Jesus Christ is one with God in addition to being equal to Him. Jesus possesses the same attributes that God possesses. Nevertheless, Jesus did not think that this equality with God was important. He stripped Himself of His divine privilege to come to earth as a *servant*. The amplification in verse 7 uses the word "slave."

Jesus came to earth as a human being who was born in the humble atmosphere of a stable where He was surrounded by animals. Jesus lived a humble life while He was growing up in Nazareth as the son of a carpenter. Jesus then humbled Himself even more by willingly dying on the cross at Calvary to pay the full price for the sins of all human beings. "...Clothe (apron) yourselves, all of you, with humility [as the garb of a servant, so that its covering cannot possibly be stripped from you, with freedom from pride and arrogance] toward one another. For God sets Himself against the proud (the insolent, the overbearing, the disdainful, the presumptuous, the boastful)—[and He opposes, frustrates, and defeats them], but gives grace (favor, blessing) to the humble." (I Peter 5:5)

God instructs every person to clothe himself or herself with humility. The word "clothe" in this sense means to *cover* yourself with humility just as the clothing you wear covers your body. You can only carry out God's will for your life to the degree that you have a servant's attitude. Your humility should be so deep that "its covering cannot possibly be stripped from you."

This verse goes on to make one of the most amazing statements in the entire Bible. You are told that God Who loves every person in the world with unconditional love (see Isaiah 54:10, John 3:16 and Romans 5:8) actually *sets Himself against* people who are proud. The amplification of this verse says that God "opposes, frustrates and defeats" proud people.

Can you even begin to imagine Almighty God setting Himself against you and defeating you? This statement shows you how much God dislikes pride. Proud people are their own little gods. They attempt to do in their lives what God desires to do. You cannot be proud and be the person God created you to be. "Therefore humble yourselves [demote, lower yourselves in your own estimation] under the mighty hand of God, that in due time He may exalt you" (I Peter 5:6)

No matter how many God-given skills, talents and abilities you may have, you are instructed to humble yourself before God and before other people. If you do, God promises to exalt you in due time. The word "exalt" means to lift up. God will lift you up in His perfect timing into a position where you are able to carry out His assignment for your life *if* you are truly humble and if you live your life with a true servant's attitude at all times.

Some people today are highly motivated to do things that they believe will cause them to receive recognition from other human beings. You saw in Chapter 3 that Jesus Christ did not seek recognition from others (see John 5:41). Humble yourself before God and before other people. "He leads the humble in what is right, and the humble He teaches His way." (Psalm 25:9)

God promises that He will guide you if you are humble. He will teach you His way. If you truly are humble, God will progressively reveal what you should do to carry out His will for your life.

God always blesses His humble and obedient children. Some of us block God from blessing us through pride and disobedience to the instructions in His Word. If you do your best to study, learn and obey the instructions in God's Word and to humble yourself before God and other people, you will place yourself in a perfect spiritual position to carry out God's plan for your life.

The Bible teaches that God is similar to a potter and that you are like clay. If you sincerely desire to carry out God's plan for your life, you will allow God to mold you, to shape you and to guide you to do what He created you to do. "...O Lord, You are our Father; we are the clay, and You our Potter, and we all are the work of Your hand." (Isaiah 64:8)

Pride always blocks God from shaping you and molding you to be what He wants you to become. "Woe to him who strives with his Maker!—a worthless piece of broken pottery among other pieces equally worthless [and yet presuming to strive with his Maker]! Shall the clay say to him who fashions it, What do you think you are making? or, Your work has no handles?" (Isaiah 45:9)

Never question what God is leading you to do. His ways are much higher and very different from the ways of human beings (see Isaiah 55:8-9). God often will call you to do things that will not make sense to the limitations of human logic and understanding.

Allow God to mold you and to shape you however He wants to mold you and shape you. "...who can resist and withstand His will? But who are you, a mere man, to criticize and contradict and answer back to God? Will what is formed say to him that formed it, Why have you made me thus? Has the potter no right over the clay, to make out of the same mass (lump) one vessel for beauty and distinction and honorable use, and another for menial or ignoble and dishonorable use?" (Romans 9:19-21)

If you do not allow God to mold you and shape you, even if what He is doing does not make sense to the limitations of your human logic and understanding, you are resisting and withstanding His will (see Proverbs 3:5-7). The clay never tells the potter how to mold it. Clay is always moldable and shapeable. God wants you to be the same.

If God calls you to do things that seem to be beneath your intelligence and abilities, do not question Him. Humble yourself before God. Humble yourself before other people. Allow God to be in control of your life as He should be (see Psalm 37:23, Proverbs 16:9 and Jeremiah 10:23).

You saw in Chapter 5 that you can block God from doing what He wants you to do with your life if you attempt to figure out what He is doing with the limitations of your human logic and understanding. Let go and let God. Trust God totally, completely and absolutely to shape you and to use you in any way that He in His infinite wisdom desires.

Does it make sense logically and intellectually that Jesus Christ would leave His exalted position in heaven where He was equal to God to come to earth as a servant to die a horrible death by crucifixion? Jesus knew that this was what God had called Him to do. He knew before He came to earth everything about the horrible suffering He would go through. Jesus was willing to humble Himself to pay this horrendous price to set *you* free from every sin you have ever committed.

Die to self. Crucify your desires. Allow God to be the Potter. Make the quality decision that your life will be like moldable clay. Allow God to use you in any way He chooses to carry out His assignment for your life.

Chapter 9

Turn Away from Personal Goals

Many people devote their lives primarily to the pursuit of pleasure. They spend large amounts of time, money and energy doing things that they perceive will give them pleasure. "He who loves pleasure will be a poor man..." (Proverbs 21:17)

Satan's demons will attempt to influence you to be selfish. They will try to deceive you in any way they can so that your life will revolve around yourself instead of revolving around serving God and other people. Satan's demons will try to whisper thoughts into your mind to influence you to pursue pleasure. They know that the Bible says that you will be spiritually poor if you pursue pleasure. You will block yourself from carrying out God's assignment for your life if you constantly pursue pleasure.

We are not saying that you should not do things that give you pleasure. We are saying that you should not allow the pursuit of pleasure to come ahead of your commitment to complete God's plan for your life. The truth is that successfully completing God's assignment for your life will give you more meaning, fulfillment and satisfaction than you will derive from pursuing selfish personal goals. "Shun youthful lusts and flee from them, and aim at and pursue righteousness (all that is virtuous and good, right living, conformity to the will of God in thought, word, and deed)…" (II Timothy 2:22)

When this verse instructs you to "shun youthful lusts," you are instructed to turn away from doing what many young people do. They are selfish in their thoughts, words and actions. You are instructed to pursue righteousness. The amplification says that righteousness includes "conformity to the will of God in thought, word and deed." You cannot successfully complete God's plan and purpose for your life if you consistently pursue pleasure the way that many immature young people do.

If you are determined to live the way that God instructs you to live, you will be highly motivated to seek, find and carry out His plan for your life. You will conform your thoughts, words and actions to doing what God created you to do.

Because Jesus Christ was born of a virgin, He is the only person who was ever born who was not a descendant of Adam. Every person, except Jesus Christ, was born with a prideful nature. We all inherit this fallen nature from our ancestor Adam.

We studied Philippians 2:21 in Chapter 4. This verse of Scripture explains that every person is born with Adam's selfish nature. You saw in Chapter 4 that, if Jesus Christ is your Savior, your life belongs to Him. Consistently turn away from the self-seeking sin nature you were born with.

Many immature people are totally committed to the pursuit of selfish goals. Having a servant's attitude and submitting to others is not natural for people who are selfish. As you grow and mature as a Christian, you will turn more and more away from the natural inclination to do what you want to do that you inherited from your ancestor Adam.

As you mature you will become increasingly motivated to follow the example of Jesus Christ by living your life with God in first place at all times, other people second and yourself last. "Whatever may be your task, work at it heartily (from the soul), as [something done] for the Lord and not for men" (Colossians 3:23)

Whatever you do, do it for the Lord. Do not put yourself ahead of Him. Keep Him in first place where He belongs. Jesus said, "…seek (aim at and strive after) first of all His kingdom and His righteousness (His way of doing and being right)…" (Matthew 6:33)

These instructions that Jesus gave to His disciples many years ago also are His instructions to you today. Strive to live in such a way that God is first at all times. Follow the example of the apostle Paul who said, "I therefore, the prisoner for the Lord, appeal to and beg you to walk (lead a life) worthy of the [divine] calling to which you have been called [with behavior that is a credit to the summons to God's service, living as becomes you] with complete lowliness of mind (humility) and meekness (unselfishness, gentleness, mildness), with patience, bearing with one another and making allowances because you love one another." (Ephesians 4:1-2)

Paul was totally committed to doing what God had called him to do. You have seen the words "prisoner," "servant" and "slave" in this chapter and in Philippians 2:7 in Chapter 8. These words are not attractive to most people, but they explain exactly what God wants you to be if you sincerely desire to carry out His assignment for your life.

Follow the example of Paul who lived with complete lowliness of mind, humility and unselfishness. Jesus told you exactly what to do to produce a rich harvest in your life. He said, "…Unless a grain of wheat falls into the earth and dies, it remains [just one grain; it never becomes more but lives] by itself alone. But if it dies, it produces many others and yields a rich harvest." (John 12:24)

Jesus spoke these words in reference to His impending crucifixion. This same principle applies to your life today. When a seed is planted, it dies by evolving from a seed into the plant that God created it to be. If you die to selfish desires, you will produce the harvest that God created you to produce with your life.

Do you have a deep and consuming desire to serve Jesus Christ? Are you like John the Baptist who said, "He must increase, but I must decrease. [He must grow more prominent; I must grow less so.]" (John 3:30)?

As you grow and mature as a Christian, your life will become increasingly devoted to serving Jesus Christ. You will willingly pay whatever price is required to complete God's assignment for your life. "…since Christ suffered in the flesh for us, for you, arm yourselves with the same thought and purpose [patiently to suffer rather than fail to please God]. For whoever has suffered in the flesh [having the mind of Christ] is done with [intentional] sin [has stopped pleasing himself and the world, and pleases God], so that he can no longer spend the rest of his natural life living by [his] human appetites and desires, but [he lives] for what God wills." (I Peter 4:1-2)

Jesus was willing to leave His exalted position in heaven to suffer by paying a tremendous price for the sins of every person. Jesus offered Himself for your sin. You are instructed to have "the same thought and purpose" that Jesus had. Turn away from selfish desires to devote your life to fulfilling God's assignment for your life.

Every sin is rooted in selfishness. Can you think of any sin that does not have selfishness as its foundation? Because this premise is true, selflessness is required to carry out God's will for your life. The psalmist David said, "Who is the man who reverently fears and worships the Lord? Him shall He teach in the way that he should choose." (Psalm 25:12)

When you fear God, you revere Him. You worship Him and hold Him in constant awe. Every aspect of your life revolves around your deep reverence for Him and your continual awareness of His indwelling presence. God will teach you and guide you to the degree that you truly fear Him.

Devote your life to using your God-given gifts and talents and your faith in God to help other people. "We who are strong [in our convictions and of robust faith] ought to bear with the failings and the frailties and the tender scruples of the weak; [we ought to help carry the doubts and qualms of others] and not to please ourselves." (Romans 15:1)

If your faith in God has increased steadily as you have matured as a Christian, use this faith to help other people who do not have strong faith in God. Center every aspect of your life around a close and intimate relationship with Jesus Christ Who lives in your heart. "...you must abide in (live in, never depart from) Him [being rooted in Him, knit to Him]..." (I John 2:27)

You are instructed to abide in Jesus. Center every aspect of your life around your commitment to Him. The amplification of this verse instructs you to be deeply rooted in Christ and to be knit to Him. Do these words describe your personal relationship with Jesus Christ? Does your life revolve around keeping Him in first place at all times? "...so that He alone in everything and in every respect might occupy the chief place [stand first and be preeminent]." (Colossians 1:18)

Please note the words "in everything," "in every respect" and "the chief place" in this verse. There is no question that you can only carry out God's assignment for your life to the degree that Jesus Christ truly is first in your life. Devote your life to serving Him and to helping other people. "...as occasion and opportunity open up to us, let us do good [morally] to all people [not only being useful or profitable to them, but also doing what is for their spiritual good and advantage]. Be mindful to be a blessing, especially to those of the household of faith [those who belong to God's family with you, the believers]." (Galatians 6:10)

Make the commitment that you will devote your life to serving Christ and to helping other people with the talents and abilities that God has given to you. Help every person you can in every way that you can, especially other members of the family of God. Use the talents and abilities that God has given to you to provide blessings to others.

This chapter instructs you to turn away from selfish desires, to revere God and to place His interests and other people ahead of the pursuit of personal goals. We now are ready to study additional instructions from the holy Scriptures that will tell you exactly what God instructs you to do to successfully carry out His assignment for your life.

Chapter 10

God Lives in Your Heart

God is omnipresent. He is able to sit on His throne in heaven and at the same time live in the heart of every person who has received Jesus Christ as his or her Savior. "One God and Father of [us] all, Who is above all [Sovereign over all], pervading all and [living] in [us] all." (Ephesians 4:6)

Please note that the word "all" is used five times in this short verse of Scripture and the amplification. If Jesus Christ is your Savior, God is your Father (see John 1:12-13, Galatians 3:26 and I John 3:1). You saw in Chapter 1 that God is omniscient. He knows every minute detail about the life of every one of the billions of people on earth. You have just seen in Ephesians 4:6 that God is omnipresent. He is able to live in the heart of every person on earth.

Is Jesus Christ your Savior? If He is, you can be certain that God is not far away from you. He lives in your heart. "[Not in your own strength] for it is God Who is all the while effectually at work in you [energizing and creating in you the power and desire], both to will and to work for His good pleasure and satisfaction and delight." (Philippians 2:13)

This verse explains that God does not want you to depend on your limited human strength and abilities. He is always working effectively *in you*. God will energize you with His supernatural power to enable you to do what He has called you to do. God wants every aspect of your life to revolve around your certainty of His indwelling presence. "…He is not far from each one of us. For in Him we live and move and have our being…" (Acts 17:27-28)

God is not far away. In addition to sitting on His throne in heaven, He lives in your heart if Jesus Christ is your Savior. Focus your life on your continual awareness of His magnificent indwelling presence. The Bible speaks of "…Him Who, by (in consequence of) the [action of His] power that is at work within us, is able to [carry out His purpose and] do superabundantly, far over and above all that we [dare] ask or think [infinitely beyond our highest prayers, desires, thoughts, hopes, or dreams]" (Ephesians 3:20)

The supernatural power of God (see I Chronicles 29:11-12, Isaiah 40:28, Jeremiah 32:17 and Luke 1:37) is available to help you carry out His assignment for your life. God is able to do in you and through you much more than you can possibly comprehend with the limitations of your human understanding.

If Jesus Christ is your Savior, you can be absolutely certain that your Father lives in your heart. You also can be certain that Jesus lives in your heart. The apostle Paul said, "I have been crucified with Christ [in Him I have shared His crucifixion]; it is no longer I who live, but Christ (the Messiah) lives in me; and the life I now live in the body I live by faith in (by adherence to and reliance on and complete trust in) the Son of God, Who loved me and gave Himself up for me." (Galatians 2:20)

The amplification in this verse says that Paul shared in the crucifixion of Jesus Christ. Paul died to his personal desires just as Jesus died to His personal desires when He was crucified. Paul explained that he no longer was in control of his life. Paul yielded control completely to Jesus Christ Who lived within him. Are you absolutely certain that Jesus Christ lives in your heart? "…Do you not yourselves realize and know [thoroughly by an ever-increasing experience] that Jesus Christ is in you…?" (II Corinthians 13:5)

The more that you meditate on Galatians 2:20, the more certain you will be that the victorious Jesus Christ *really does* live in your heart. You will be constantly aware of His ind- welling presence. "May Christ through your faith [actually] dwell (settle down, abide, make His permanent home) in your hearts!..." (Ephesians 3:17)

You have seen that God lives in your heart. You have seen that Jesus Christ lives in your heart. The Bible also teaches that the Holy Spirit lives in the heart of every person who has received Jesus Christ as his or her Savior. "…God's Spirit has His permanent dwelling in you [to be at home in you, collectively as a church and also individually]..." (I Corinthians 3:16)

The Holy Spirit is omnipresent just as God and Jesus are omnipresent. Please note the word "permanent dwelling" in this verse. When we studied Ephesians 3:17, the words "per- manent home" were used in the amplification to emphasize that Jesus Christ lives permanently in your heart. You can be absolutely certain that God your Father, Jesus Christ and the Holy Spirit make their permanent dwelling in *your* heart.

God never intended for you to carry out His plan for your life by depending on your limited human abilities (see Psalm 24:11, Isaiah 2:27 and II Corinthians 1:8-9 and 3:5). If Jesus Christ is your Savior, you are a spiritual powerhouse. "…in Him the whole fullness of Deity (the Godhead) continues to dwell in bodily form [giving complete expression of the di- vine nature]. And you are in Him, made full and having come to fullness of life [in Christ you too are filled with the Godhead—Father, Son and Holy Spirit—and reach full spiritual stature]...." (Colossians 2:9-10)

Please note that the words "the Godhead" are used twice in the amplification of this passage of Scripture. The Godhead is described in verse 10 as Father, Son and Holy Spirit. God has fully equipped you with *everything* you will ever need to carry out His assignment for your life. He has taken up residence in your heart. His Son Jesus Christ makes His permanent home in your heart. The Holy Spirit makes His permanent home in your heart.

No matter how difficult the assignment that God has given to you might seem, you can be absolutely *certain* that you have within yourself everything you will ever need to solve every problem you will ever face in carrying out God's assignment for your life. Center your life around your absolute certainty that God the Father, Jesus Christ and the Holy Spirit live in *your* heart.

If you have a deep and sincere desire to seek, find and carry out God's plan for your life, focus continually on your certainty that the Godhead – Father, Son and Holy Spirit – lives in your heart. The kingdom of God is not located only in heaven. When you received Jesus Christ as your Savior, God placed His entire kingdom *within you*. Jesus said, "...the kingdom of God is within you [in your hearts]..." (Luke 17:21)

There is no question that God has placed *everything* within you that you will ever need to carry out His assignment for your life. If you know that you are doing what God has called you to do and you face severe adversity, meditate on the Scripture in this chapter. Do not allow any problem, no matter how difficult it may seem, to concern you. The same words that Jesus spoke to His disciples many years ago apply to you today. Jesus said, "…With men this is impossible, but all things are possible with God." (Matthew 19:26)

Chapter 11

You Can Hear the Voice of God

If you deeply and sincerely desire to carry out God's assignment for your life, you will need to know how to hear God's voice. You have seen that God has a plan for the life of every person on earth. He will reveal exactly what He wants you to do. God will not send you a letter or an email to explain His assignment. He will not call you on the phone. If you learn how to hear God's voice, you will constantly receive revelation from within yourself as to what God wants you to do and how to do it.

Hearing the voice of God can be compared to tuning in to a radio station or television channel. In the atmosphere around you at this time, radio and television programming is being broadcast. However, you cannot hear what is being said unless you tune in to a specific radio station or television channel.

God is omnipresent. You saw in Ephesians 4:6 in the last chapter that God is able to have individual conversations with billions of people throughout the world at the same time. God speaks to you throughout every day of your life. Unfortunately, many Christians live, die and go to heaven without ever hearing God's voice.

If Jesus Christ is your Savior, God has given you the ability to hear what He is saying to you. Jesus said, "Whoever is of God listens to God. [Those who belong to God hear the words of God.]…" (John 8:47)

When Jesus speaks of whoever is of God, He refers to every person who is a member of the family of God. You became a member of the family of God on the day you were saved (see John 1:12-13, II Corinthians 6:18, Galatians 3:26 and I John 3:1). Every member of God's family is given the ability to hear His voice.

In this book we are speaking specifically of hearing God in regard to carrying out His assignment for your life. God also speaks to you in other areas throughout every day of your life. You can learn how to hear and understand what God is saying to you just as children on earth learn how to understand what their parents are saying. Jesus said, "…Everyone who is of the Truth [who is a friend of the Truth, who belongs to the Truth] hears and listens to My voice." (John 18:37)

This verse and the amplification refer to "the Truth" three times. When Jesus speaks of the Truth, He speaks of the Word of God (see John 17:17). He also speaks of Himself (see John 14:6) and of the Holy Spirit (see John 14:17 and 16:13).

If you faithfully obey God's instructions to renew your mind by studying His Word each day (see II Corinthians 4:16, Ephesians 4:23 and II Timothy 2:15) and by meditating day and night on the holy Scriptures (see Joshua 1:8 and Psalm 1:2-3), you are constantly tuning in to the voice of God. The more you get into the Word of God and the more you get the Word of God into yourself, the more you will be able to hear God's voice.

You just saw in John 18:37 that Christians can hear God speaking to them. Take full advantage of the privilege that you have been given to hear God's voice. Listen carefully to Him each day as He guides you to do what He has called you to do. Jesus said, "He who has ears [to hear], let him be listening and let him consider and perceive and comprehend by hearing." (Matthew 13:9)

If Jesus Christ is your Savior, you have ears to hear. You have been given the ability to hear God's voice. Listen continually. *Expect* to hear God speaking to you. "…your ears will hear a word behind you, saying, This is the way; walk in it, when you turn to the right hand and when you turn to the left." (Isaiah 30:21)

The words "behind you" are used here because this is an Old Testament verse. The Old Testament consistently teaches that God is with you. As you saw in the last chapter, the New Testament teaches that God lives in you.

God lives in your heart. He speaks to you continually. He will tell you what to do and how to do it. He will tell you when to turn to the right and when to turn to the left. Your loving Father is speaking to you throughout every day of your life. He will tell you exactly what to do to carry out His assignment for your life. "Incline your ear [submit and consent to the divine will]…" (Isaiah 55:3)

The words "incline your ear" mean to tune in to the voice of God. The amplification in this verse instructs you to "submit and consent" to God's will for your life. Do whatever your Father tells you to do. "He delivers the afflicted in their affliction and opens their ears [to His voice] in adversity." (Job 36:15)

God promises to deliver you when you face adversity. His Word says that He will open your ears to His voice when you face adversity. Expect to hear God speaking to you when you face adversity. Be like the psalmist who said, "I will listen [with expectancy] to what God the Lord will say..." (Psalm 85:8)

God has been speaking to you today. He spoke to you yesterday, last week, last month and last year. He has spoken to you throughout every day of your life. You have had the ability to hear what He is saying to you since the day you received Jesus Christ as your Savior.

In Chapter 6 we studied several verses of Scripture that instruct you to turn away from the world. Get out of the natural realm. Get into the supernatural realm. *Know* that God speaks to you every day of your life. Learn how to hear His voice.

You have seen that God lives in your heart if Jesus Christ is your Savior. God does not have to speak loudly to you. He usually speaks very softly. The prophet Elijah explained that God's voice is "...[a sound of gentle stillness and] a still, small voice." (I Kings 19:12)

God is the greatest power in the entire universe. He can speak very loudly if He so chooses (see Job 37:2-4 and John 12:9). However, God does not speak loudly to you when He lives inside of you. Usually He will speak to you in "a still, small voice."

You will block yourself from hearing God's voice whenever you are agitated for any reason. If you are tense, worried, angry or if any other negative emotion prevails in your life, you will block yourself from hearing God Who speaks softly. You will only hear what God is saying if you are calm, quiet and confident. "...be calm and cool and steady, accept and suffer unflinchingly every hardship..." (II Timothy 4:5)

These words that Paul spoke to Timothy are God's words to you. God instructs you to face adversity calmly and quietly because you have absolute faith that He will bring you safely through adversity as He repeatedly promises to do (see Psalms 46:1 and 50:14 and Isaiah 43:2-3).

If you are *certain* that God will bring you through adversity, you will not become agitated when you face problems. If you consistently study and meditate on the Word of God, your Father will teach you how to remain calm during adversity. "Blessed (happy, fortunate, to be envied) is the man whom You discipline and instruct, O Lord, and teach out of Your law, that You may give him power to keep himself calm in the days of adversity…" (Psalm 94:12-13)

If you focus continually on God and His Word instead of focusing on the severity of whatever problems you face, God will teach you. He will give you the ability to remain calm and peaceful when you face adversity. "You will guard him and keep him in perfect and constant peace whose mind [both its inclination and its character] is stayed on You, because he commits himself to You, leans on You, and hopes confidently in You." (Isaiah 26:3)

Your Father promises to "guard you and keep you in perfect and constant peace." How do you receive this awesome blessing from God? You receive this blessing by keeping your mind *stayed* on God at all times because you are committed to Him and because you have absolute faith in Him.

In this chapter we have given you several verses of Scripture about hearing the voice of God. If you would like to learn more about how to hear God's voice, we recommend our book, *You Can Hear the Voice of God.* This book is solidly anchored on 286 verses of Scripture with a simple and easy-to-understand explanation of each verse. (See the order form in the back of this book. You also can order on our website: lamplight.net or call 1-800-540-1597.)

Chapter 12

God Will Guide You Continually

If you consistently seek God's will for your life, you can be certain that God will guide you every step of the way. He said, "I [the Lord] will instruct you and teach you in the way you should go; I will counsel you with My eye upon you." (Psalm 32:8)

God promises to instruct you and to teach you. He will show you exactly what to do. He is watching over you at all times. Omnipresent God can keep His eye on you at the same time that He is looking at billions of other people. God wants you to successfully complete His assignment for your life. He is very interested in everything you do to achieve this goal. "The steps of a [good] man are directed and established by the Lord when He delights in his way [and He busies Himself with his every step]." (Psalm 37:23)

The words "a good man" in this verse refer to any man or woman who is good before God because he or she is righteous because Jesus Christ has paid the price for all of his or her sins. If Jesus Christ is your Savior, God will direct you throughout your life. He is delighted when you fervently seek His plan for your life. He pays close attention to everything you do. He will help you with every detail of what He has called you to do. "…the Lord shall guide you continually…" (Isaiah 58:11)

God does not promise to guide you some of the time or most of the time. He promises to guide you *continually*. If you learn how to hear His voice and if you consistently turn to Him for guidance, He will give you the guidance that you need to carry out every aspect of His assignment for your life. "…God is our God forever and ever; He will be our guide [even] until death." (Psalm 48:14)

God promises to guide you right up until the moment you die and go to be with Him in heaven. He will guide you if you turn to Him continually. Be like the psalmist who said, "…I am continually with You; You do hold my right hand. You will guide me with Your counsel…" (Psalm 73:23-24)

Do you remember how secure you felt as a child when you were walking with one or both of your parents and your mother and/or your father held your hand? You will experience this security supernaturally if you continually turn to your Father for guidance in carrying out His assignment for your life. "…you do not know [the least thing] about what may happen tomorrow. What is the nature of your life? You are [really] but a wisp of vapor (a puff of smoke, a mist) that is visible for a little while and then disappears [into thin air]. You ought instead to say, If the Lord is willing, we shall live and we shall do this or that [thing]." (James 4:14-15)

If your life is devoted to doing what God has called you to do, you will not worry about the future. You do not know what will happen in the future, but God does. You saw in Psalm 48:14 that God promises to guide you throughout every day of your life. Jesus Christ said, "…when He, the Spirit of Truth (the Truth-giving Spirit) comes, He will guide you into all the Truth (the whole, full Truth). For He will not speak His own message [on His own authority]; but He will tell whatever He hears [from the Father; He will give the message that has been given to Him], and He will announce and declare to you the things that are to come [that will happen in the future]." (John 16:13)

Jesus spoke these words to His disciples, referring to the Holy Spirit coming upon them after He was crucified. The Holy Spirit comes into the life of every person who receives Jesus Christ as his or her Savior (see Galatians 4:6). If Jesus is your Savior, you can be certain that the Holy Spirit Who lives in your heart will guide you to do exactly what God has called you to do.

The Holy Spirit knows exactly what will take place in the future. He will guide you now to make correct decisions based on what He knows will happen in the months and years to come. Do not make decisions without receiving continual guidance from the Holy Spirit. Be like the apostle Paul who said, "…I do not run uncertainly (without definite aim)…." (I Corinthians 9:26)

The Holy Spirit will give you the specific and exact instructions that you need to carry out God's assignment for your life. "…walk and live [habitually] in the [Holy] Spirit [responsive to and controlled and guided by the Spirit]…" (Galatians 5:16)

Please note the word "habitually" in the amplification of this verse. When you do something habitually, you do whatever you are doing constantly. Do not attempt to control your life. Allow the Holy Spirit to guide you every step of the way. "If we live by the [Holy] Spirit, let us also walk by the Spirit. [If by the Holy Spirit we have our life in God, let us go forward walking in line, our conduct controlled by the Spirit.]" (Galatians 5:25)

This verse and the amplification instruct you to live by the Holy Spirit, walk by the Spirit and to be controlled by the

Spirit. "…you are living the life of the Spirit, if the [Holy] Spirit of God [really] dwells within you [directs and controls you]…." (Romans 8:9)

The Holy Spirit will guide you one step at a time. Take the next step that He reveals to you. Trust Him to show you where to go from there. "…The God of our forefathers has destined and appointed you to come progressively to know His will [to perceive, to recognize more strongly and clearly, and to become better and more intimately acquainted with His will]…" (Acts 22:14)

The word "progressively" means that something is done is successive steps. Do not expect to know from the beginning every detail about what God has called you to do. He usually will show you the big picture of what He wants you to do. He then will progressively reveal the details to you if you consistently persevere in seeking His plan. Willingly surrender your life to the Holy Spirit. "Do not quench (suppress or subdue) the [Holy] Spirit" (I Thessalonians 5:19)

God has a wonderful plan for your life. Do not block the Holy Spirit by consistently pursuing personal goals. Be willing to serve your apprenticeship. Be willing to do the little things that God will call you to do when you begin pursuing His assignment for your life.

Do not consider small jobs to be menial. Do not consider them beneath you. Do everything that God calls you to do to the best of your ability because you have a servant's heart.

Jesus explained this principle through a parable about a wealthy man who sent ten of his servants out to carry out different assignments. This man required his servants to do little things. When the first servant came back with a good report, this man said, "…Well done, excellent bond servant! Because you have been faithful and trustworthy in a very little [thing], you shall have authority over ten cities." (Luke 19:17)

This same principle applies to carrying out God's assignment for your life. If you are faithful in doing the little things well, God will reward your commitment by giving you greater responsibilities.

Refuse to be impatient. Trust God to reveal the details of His plan for your life in His perfect timing. Trust God's timing just as you trust Him in every other area. "To everything there is a season, and a time for every matter or purpose under heaven" (Ecclesiastes 3:1)

God has a specific time for everything. He knows exactly how He wants to unfold His plan for your life. Do not attempt to figure everything out with the limitations of your human logic and intellectual reasoning. God will give you the big picture. Move forward steadily, trusting Him one day at a time. Jesus said, "...do not worry or be anxious about tomorrow, for tomorrow will have worries and anxieties of its own. Sufficient for each day is its own trouble." (Matthew 6:34)

The Word of God repeatedly instructs you to live your life one day at a time. This principle is especially important in regard to God's assignment for your life. "Blessed be the Lord, Who bears our burdens and carries us day by day..." (Psalm 68:19)

Do not struggle and strain. Trust God completely to carry *both* you and any burdens you face one day at a time. "...as your day, so shall your strength, your rest and security, be." (Deuteronomy 33:25)

God will give you the strength that you need to get through today. He instructs you to rest in Him. Turn to God for security instead of trusting in worldly sources of security. "...he who has once entered [God's] rest also has ceased from [the weariness and pain] of human labors..." (Hebrews 4:10)

This verse and the amplification explain exactly what to do when you rest in God. Turn completely away from "the weariness and pain of human labors." Trust God to do in you, through you and for you what He has called you to do with your life.

Trust God completely to progressively reveal His will to you. Rest in Him. Your Father will work everything out if you will move forward patiently one day at a time, trusting Him completely every step of the way.

Chapter 13

Experience Great Fulfillment As You Grow Older

I will begin this chapter by doing something that I very seldom do. This chapter will begin with my opinion that is not directly supported by Scripture. I am now 81 years old. I am certain that I have been in the center of God's will for my life for the past 30 years. I wrote my first Christian book 30 years ago and I have written 26 additional books since then (14 of these books were co-authored with Judy).

As I have grown older in recent years, very few days go by where I am not acutely conscious that I am in the center of God's will for my life. My life is much more meaningful and fulfilling than it would be if these final years of my life were devoted to the pursuit of pleasure.

The Bible does not say that God's assignment for your life is directed at any particular age. In my opinion, the people who very much need to seek, find and carry out God's plan for their lives are Christians whose children have grown up and gone out to develop families of their own.

If you and your spouse are Christians and if you are doing your best to develop your marriage and to raise your children according to God's instructions in these areas, you definitely are in the center of God's will for your life. I am not saying that Christian parents who are raising children cannot be carrying out God's plan for their lives in any other area in addition to their families. However, many Christian parents who are raising children based on scriptural instructions are in the center of God's will for that area of their lives. They experience great joy, meaning and fulfillment because their families are growing based on God's specific instructions to husbands and wives for raising their children.

On the other hand, many unbelievers and Christians who are not developing their marriages and raising their children according to God's instructions inevitably will experience significant family problems. Our newspapers contain many stories of rebellious teenagers who are living far away from God's instructions. Divorce is rampant in the world today. Christian parents who want to find God's will for their lives should be highly motivated to learn and obey God's specific instructions to husbands, wives and parents.

We will not devote this chapter to these instructions. Christian bookstores contain many books explaining God's instructions for families. We want to devote the beginning of this chapter to life after the children are raised and gone out on their own. If there ever is a time when Christians should diligently pursue the scriptural instructions in this book pertaining to God's assignment for their lives, I believe that this time begins with the period of time after your children are grown up.

Your relationship with your spouse is a lifetime relationship. Your relationship with your children does not end when they leave your home. Many parents still spend a great deal of time with their children and grandchildren. However, you will spend much less time with your children than you did when they were growing up. You will have increasing amounts of discretionary time after your children are grown up and leave your home.

All of our children have grown up and gone out on their own. Our children and grandchildren live in Florida (100 miles away), North Carolina, New Hampshire, California, Oregon and Tennessee. Judy and I enjoy watching our children growing and maturing as parents. We enjoy watching our grandchildren grow up. In addition, we are being fulfilled by doing what God has called us to do with Lamplight Ministries.

The words "midlife crisis" have evolved during our generation. Many people come to the stage where their children have grown and are out on their own. Midlife crisis begins when people realize that they are in the last half of their lives and they are not experiencing the fulfillment and meaning that they experienced when their children were growing up.

Midlife crisis has its roots in the lack of fulfillment that is experienced by people whose lives are devoted primarily to pursuing personal goals. This lack of fulfillment can only be overcome by having a deep and sincere desire to find and complete God's plan for your life.

The next period of life after the time when children grow up and leave your home is what the world calls retirement years. Retirement is a worldly concept, not a biblical concept. The world proclaims how great the retirement years will be and how enjoyable the pursuit of pleasure will be as a well-earned reward for many years of hard work. To a degree, this premise is true. However, if you are in or approaching your retirement years and the pursuit of pleasure is your primary goal, you will experience significant emptiness in your life.

Once again, there is nothing wrong with enjoying your life, but you will make a big mistake, in my opinion, if you place anything ahead of seeking, finding and carrying out God's assignment for your life. Many people put the pursuit of pleasure ahead of God. Other people place the accumulation of wealth ahead of God.

You saw in Chapter 9 that the Bible says that the pursuit of wealth and the pursuit of pleasure will not provide meaning and fulfillment in your life. "...turn not aside from following the Lord, but serve Him with all your heart. And turn not aside after vain and worthless things which cannot profit or deliver you, for they are empty and futile." (I Samuel 12:20-21)

The Bible instructs you to serve God with all your heart. You are instructed not to devote your life primarily to the pursuit of "vain and worthless" things in the world that are "empty and futile."

The fulfillment that some people experience from their secular employment disappears when they reach retirement age. Many people learn the hard way as they grow older that the fulfillment they previously experienced in raising their families and in their vocation is gone.

Spiritually mature Christians understand that, if there ever is a time to focus on the pursuit of God's will for their lives, these years are that time. "...stand firm and mature [in spiritual growth], convinced and fully assured in everything willed by God." (Colossians 4:12)

God knows exactly where you are in your life. He knows every challenge that you face. He allowed you to come to this point in your life. If you are paying the price of renewing your mind in the Scripture contained in this book, you will pursue eternal goals. You will become increasingly focused on seeking, finding and carrying out God's plan for your life.

Many people experience significant health challenges as they reach the final years of their lives. We believe that Christians who seek and find God's assignment will live much longer on the whole and be healthier than people of the same age whose lives are primarily devoted to the pursuit of personal goals.

I am 81 years old as I write this book. Judy is 74. I have some minor health challenges, but I am not under a doctor's care. I do not take any prescriptions. Judy is very healthy. She also does not take any medication.

I can tell you from personal experience that my life today would be very frustrating if I did not spend most of my declining energy on God's assignment for my life. Many older people are increasingly preoccupied with their health challenges. Their lives revolve around whatever health challenges they face and an aimless pursuit of pleasure because they do not know what else to do with their lives.

Judy and I work side by side each day pursuing God's will for our lives. We are very fulfilled by what God has called us to do in Lamplight Ministries. As this book is written, we have received comments from people in 61 countries stating that our books and Scripture Meditation Cards have helped them. During these final years of my life, I am delighted that I am pursuing God's will each day instead of focusing on health challenges and the pursuit of secular pleasure.

If you are in your retirement years, we encourage you to take a good look at yourself. Are you experiencing deep meaning and fulfillment in your life? Are you fervently pursuing God's assignment for your life? If not, you could be reading this book because God has led you to it. The scriptural instructions in this book could be exactly what you need at this stage of your life.

The older you are, the more important it is to be in the center of God's will. You will experience great meaning, joy and fulfillment during your final years if you are doing what God has called you to do instead of devoting most of your energy to the pursuit of personal goals. Jesus Christ said, "Blessed (happy—with life-joy and satisfaction in God's favor and salvation, apart from your outward condition— and to be envied) are you who hunger and seek with eager desire now, for you shall be filled and completely satisfied!..." (Luke 6:21)

This verse of Scripture explains that God will bless you with happiness, joy, satisfaction, meaning and fulfillment if you eagerly seek Him and His plan for your life. If you hunger to know God and to find and carry out His assignment for your life, you will experience fulfillment, meaning and satisfaction.

God placed the need for eternal significance in your heart when He created you. "…He also has planted eternity in men's hearts and minds [a divinely implanted sense of a purpose working through the ages which nothing under the sun but God alone can satisfy]…" (Ecclesiastes 3:11)

God created you in such a way that nothing in the world, except completing His assignment for your life, will give you complete satisfaction, meaning and fulfillment. If you do not have an eternal perspective and your life revolves around the things of the world, you will experience increasing dissatisfaction as you grow older.

We studied several verses of Scripture in Chapter 2 that explained the eternal significance of completing God's assignment for your life. The amplification in Ecclesiastes 3:11 says that God will satisfy the "divinely implanted sense of a purpose working through the ages" in your life.

Jesus Christ died on the cross to pay the full price for your sins. He also died to set you free from the worldliness that is so prevalent in our generation. Turn away from the world. Turn away from the pursuit of sensual worldly goals. "...The eye is not satisfied with seeing, nor the ear filled with hearing." (Ecclesiastes 1:8)

Some older people who are frustrated with the emptiness of their lives say to themselves, "Is this all there is?" No, God has provided much more for each of us. God has made it possible for you to experience deep meaning, satisfaction and fulfillment that cannot be experienced through the pursuit of sensual worldly goals.

True fulfillment comes from the inside out, not from the outside in. People who consistently pursue worldly goals are doomed to a life of ultimate frustration. "...[the lust of] the eyes of man is never satisfied." (Proverbs 27:20)

Many retired people devote their lives to the pursuit of pleasure. Their lives are relatively idle. They spend a great deal of time watching television. They pursue various worldly goals that become more and more unfulfilling as the years go by.

Your final years can be the *best years of your life* if you turn away from the pursuit of empty worldly goals to devote your life to doing what God has called you to do. Turn away from the vain and worthless things of the world that cannot provide meaning, fulfillment and satisfaction in your life. Study and meditate on the Scripture in this book to learn what God has called you to do. Obey these instructions from God. (We also recommend our book titled *God's Instructions for Growing Older.*)

There is much more to life than many older people experience. God's plan for your life is very important at any age, but if you are in the final years of your life, make the quality decision that you will *eagerly* seek the assignment that God has given to you.

The life of Dr. Albert Schweitzer is an excellent example of a godly man who dedicated the final years of his life to serving God and other human beings. Dr. Schweitzer turned away from the worldly riches he could have received as a successful surgeon. Instead, he went into the African jungle where God had called him to go to devote his life to helping lepers.

This decision does not make sense from a worldly perspective. Dr. Schweitzer said, "The only ones among you who will be happy are those who have sought and found how to serve. The interior joy we feel when we have done a good deed, when we feel we have been needed somewhere and have lent a helping hand is the nourishment the soul requires. I have no intention of dying so long as I can do things for God. If I keep doing these things, there is no need to die so I will live a long, long time."

I can identify completely with what Dr. Schweitzer said. At the age of 81 I am very excited about the next ten books that I know God has called me to write (and the probability of additional books after that). I experience continual fulfillment from the letters and emails that come in from all over the world from people who have been helped by our books and Scripture cards.

I can tell you from personal experience that devoting the final years of my life to God's plan for my life is *very* meaningful and fulfilling. God has a definite and specific plan for your life. Seek this plan wholeheartedly.

Martin Luther was a Christian leader who understood the relationship between the will of God and experiencing the joy of the Lord. Martin Luther said, "Blessed is he who submits to the will of God; he can never be unhappy."

You will never be unhappy if you are in the center of God's will for your life. In the next chapter we will study several verses of Scripture pertaining to fulfillment in your life, living a long life and being fruitful in your old age.

Chapter 14

The Final Years of Your Life

God wants each person He creates to experience meaning, satisfaction and fulfillment in his or her life. "…a good man shall be satisfied with [the fruit of] his ways [with the holy thoughts and actions which his heart prompts and in which he delights]." (Proverbs 14:14)

The words a "good man" in this verse refer to a person who is good in God's sight. If Jesus Christ is your Savior, you are a good man (or woman) in God's sight. Jesus has paid the full price for all of your sins. You have been completely cleansed from all sin.

If Jesus Christ is your Savior, you will experience meaning, satisfaction and fulfillment to the degree that your thoughts and actions are based on the ways of God. You will be satisfied and fulfilled if you consistently live in the center of God's will for your life. "…He satisfies the longing soul and fills the hungry soul with good." (Psalm 107:9)

God will give you great satisfaction if you long to live your life the way He wants you to live. If you hunger to carry out His assignment for your life, your Father will give you supernatural meaning, satisfaction and fulfillment.

In Chapter 1 we studied Jeremiah 1:5 and Psalm 139:16. These verses of Scripture indicate that God had a specific plan for each day in the lives of the prophet Jeremiah and the psalmist David before He created either of them in their mother's womb. God also had a specific plan for every day of your life before He created you. The psalmist David said, "He will fulfill the desires of those who reverently and worshipfully fear Him..." (Psalm 145:19)

If you fear God, you revere Him. Your attitude toward Him is an attitude of constant reverence and awe. Every aspect of your life will revolve around your absolute certainty of His magnificent indwelling presence.

If you truly fear God, you will be committed to seeking, finding and carrying out His plan for your life. As you grow older, you will become more and more dedicated to devote the remainder of your life to doing what God has called you to do. "...your old men shall dream [divinely suggested] dreams." (Acts 2:17)

The amplification of this verse states that old men (and women) will dream "divinely suggested" dreams. Your dreams will come from God if you are an older person and you are totally committed to doing what God has called you to do with your life. Your Father will nourish this desire through your dreams. These dreams often will indicate some aspect of His plan for your life.

We now will study several verses of Scripture pertaining to living a long life. God created you to live a long, meaningful and full life. Eliphaz counseled Job, "You shall come to your grave in ripe old age..." (Job 5:26)

The words "ripe old age" in this verse indicate, according to Eliphaz, that you will be healthy and productive up to the time of your death. I pray daily that I will be able to write every day throughout the remainder of my life up to the day that I go to be with God in heaven. At the age of 81 I am consumed with completing the assignment that God has given to me. I immerse myself day and night in His Word. "Hear, O my son, and receive my sayings, and the years of your life shall be many." (Proverbs 4:10)

The words that King Solomon spoke to his son are God's words to you. If you consistently study and meditate on God's Word and you faithfully obey God's instructions, you will live a long and a full life. "...by me [Wisdom from God] your days shall be multiplied, and the years of your life shall be increased." (Proverbs 9:11)

If you truly seek God's will, your life will be yielded to Him. You will constantly hear Him speaking to you (see John 8:47 and 18:37). You will live a long and a full life if you are doing what God in His wisdom instructs you to do. "...if a man should live many years, let him rejoice in them all..." (Ecclesiastes 11:8)

Enjoy your life to the fullest. The final years of your life will be very fulfilling if you are doing what God created you to do. God did not create you to spend these years pursuing worldly goals. God created you to live these years in total commitment to carrying out His assignment for your life. Be like the psalmist who prayed saying, "...even when I am old and gray-headed, O God, forsake me not, [but keep me alive] until I have declared Your mighty strength to [this] generation, and Your might and power to all that are to come." (Psalm 71:18)

The psalmist prayed asking God to keep him alive until he completed the assignment that God had given to him. We pray that the scriptural contents of this book will inspire you to be like the psalmist who said, "I shall not die but live, and shall declare the works and recount the illustrious acts of the Lord." (Psalm 118:17)

God's plan for your life is important at all times, but I have found that God's plan is especially important during these final years of my life. I first started teaching a Bible study in our church almost 40 years ago. I taught the Bible study in this church and in several seminars that I gave in the United States and Canada.

I wrote my first Christian book 30 years ago. This is Book #27. I am totally committed to completing God's assignment during the remainder of my life. "[Growing in grace] they shall still bring forth fruit in old age; they shall be full of sap [of spiritual vitality] and [rich in the] verdure [of trust, love, and contentment]." (Psalm 92:14)

God will give you grace to produce supernatural fruit during your final years if you are completely dedicated to carrying out His assignment for your life. You will be filled with spiritual vitality. You will experience great contentment and fulfillment during your final years if your life is dedicated to doing what God has called you to do. You will be like the apostle Paul who referred to himself as "…an ambassador [of Christ Jesus] and an old man and now a prisoner for His sake also" (Philemon 1:9)

An ambassador represents one country to another country. If your life is surrendered to Jesus Christ and you are doing what God created you to do, you are an ambassador of Jesus Christ. You represent Jesus by doing what God has called you to do with your life (see Ephesians 2:10).

True freedom in the spiritual realm comes in the last place where people would expect to find freedom. Carnal people think that freedom comes from doing whatever they want to do. God's ways are very different from the ways of the world (see Isaiah 55:8-9). God created you in such a way that you will only experience freedom through *surrender*. "Now the Lord is the Spirit, and where the Spirit of the Lord is, there is liberty (emancipation from bondage, freedom)." (II Corinthians 3:17)

Jesus Christ set you free from the bondage that enslaves many people in the world. True liberty in the spiritual realm comes from doing what the Holy Spirit leads you to do instead of consistently pursuing personal desires. "...live and move not in the ways of the flesh but in the ways of the Spirit [our lives governed not by the standards and according to the dictates of the flesh, but controlled by the Holy Spirit]." (Romans 8:4)

The older you become, the more important it is for you to get out of the driver's seat. Consistently yield control of your life to the Holy Spirit. You do not have a lot of time remaining. Use this time wisely. Do not waste the precious final years of your life.

Some Christians are spiritually blind. They cannot understand the heavy load that they carry if they go through life carrying the burden of selfish goals and desires. If you get rid of this heavy burden by consistently doing what God has called you to do, the quality of your life will improve tremendously. The most exciting place where you can possibly be is in the center of God's will for your life.

Some Christians look at success from a worldly perspective. Success from God's eternal perspective has nothing to do with being famous in the world or the accumulation of wealth. True success from God's perspective comes from cheerfully surrendering control of your life to do what He created you to do.

You saw in Chapter 4 that your life belongs to Jesus Christ. Jesus paid a tremendous price for you. Surrender control of your life to Him. Receive the deep meaning, satisfaction and fulfillment that God will give you if your life is surrendered to Christ and you are completely devoted to doing what God created you to do with your life.

Chapter 15

Total Commitment to God's Assignment for Your Life

The scriptural instruction in the first 14 chapters of this book could be life-changing to many readers. We believe that many people who read these chapters will find that they are filled with supernatural scriptural truth that will have a great impact on their lives. There is no question that God has a definite plan for your life. We pray that you are highly motivated to seek, find and successfully complete God's assignment for your life.

God's will for your life can be compared to a narrow road. Many people are on the wide road of pursuing their personal desires. They are not aware that the narrow road of God's will exists.

Getting on the wide road is easy. Most people are on the wide road of doing what they want to do. If you are not absolutely certain that you already are on the narrow road, we believe that the Truth from God's Word in this book will help you to get on the narrow road and stay there. Jesus Christ said, "Enter through the narrow gate; for wide is the gate and spacious and broad is the way that leads away to destruction, and many are those who are entering through it.

But the gate is narrow (contracted by pressure) and the way is straitened and compressed that leads away to life, and few are those who find it." (Matthew 7:13-14)

Jesus speaks of the wide road leading to destruction. He refers here to people who do not receive Him as Savior and are headed on the wide road that ultimately will lead to suffering throughout eternity in hell (see Revelation 20:15). Everyone who has not received Jesus Christ as his or her Savior is on the wide road. You can only travel on the narrow road that leads to glorious eternal life in heaven if Jesus Christ is your Savior.

This same principle applies to the remainder of your life on earth. If you know that you are on the narrow road to glorious eternal life in heaven, will you commit to the narrow road of God's assignment for the remainder of your life on earth?

We emphasized in Chapter 4 and again in the last chapter that your life belongs to Jesus Christ if He is your Savior (see Romans 14:7-8 and I Corinthians 5:14-15 and 6:19-20). The same principle that applies to the narrow road of where you will spend eternity applies to the remainder of your life on earth. Your Father wants you to learn His assignment for your life. He wants you to be totally committed to carrying out His assignment. "Delight yourself also in the Lord, and He will give you the desires and secret petitions of your heart." (Psalm 37:4)

God wants you to delight in Him. If you are delighted about someone or something, you have great joy in that person or thing. We pray that the scriptural instructions in the first 14 chapters of this book have given you great motivation to complete God's assignment for your life. If you are delighted in God, He will give you the secret desires of your heart because your desires for the remainder of your life and His desires for you will be the same.

In Chapter 3 we studied Scripture where Jesus Christ referred to Himself as a servant. If Jesus Christ Who is equal to God looked at Himself as a servant, there is no question that God wants every person to have the attitude of being a servant in regard to carrying out His assignment for his or her life.

God wants you to be completely committed to doing what He has called you to do with your life. "Never lag in zeal and in earnest endeavor; be aglow and burning with the Spirit, serving the Lord." (Romans 12:11)

Your Father instructs you not to lag in zeal. When you are zealous about something, you are enthusiastic and excited. You are totally committed. You are instructed to be "aglow and burning with the Spirit" as you serve the Lord.

You have seen that Jesus was totally committed to carrying out God's will during His earthly ministry (see John 5:30). Make the commitment now that you also will be totally committed to doing what God has called you to do with your life. "...offer and yield yourselves to God as though you have been raised from the dead to [perpetual] life, and your bodily members [and faculties] to God, presenting them as implements of righteousness." (Romans 6:13)

You are instructed to yield yourself to God just as you will yield to Him throughout eternity in heaven. The reason that you are still here on earth after you are saved is to complete God's assignment for your life.

We studied Ephesians 2:10 in Chapter 1. We now will look again at this verse from the perspective of what we are studying in this chapter. "...we are God's [own] handiwork (His workmanship), recreated in Christ Jesus, [born anew] that we may do those good works which God predestined (planned beforehand) for us [taking paths which He prepared ahead of time], that we should walk in them [living the good life which He prearranged and made ready for us to live]." (Ephesians 2:10)

If Jesus Christ is your Savior, God has a definite plan for the remainder of your life on earth. This verse explains that God has specific paths for you to walk on that He prearranged for you. Make the total commitment that you will enthusiastically and wholeheartedly seek the narrow road of the path that God has laid out for the remainder of your life. "See that you discharge carefully [the duties of] the ministry and fulfill the stewardship which you have received in the Lord." (Colossians 4:17)

Please note the word "stewardship" in this verse. A steward is someone who commits to doing something for another person. Make the commitment that you will fulfill the stewardship that God has given to you. Be like the apostle Paul who said, "...be firm (steadfast), immovable, always abounding in the work of the Lord [always being superior, excelling, doing more than enough in the service of the Lord], knowing and being continually aware that your labor in the Lord is not futile [it is never wasted or to no purpose]." (I Corinthians 15:58)

The ministry of the apostle Paul was characterized by his total commitment. Your Father wants you to have a similar commitment to what He has called you to do. You are instructed to be "immovable." This instruction means that you should be *so* committed to doing what God has called you to do that you will not allow anything to deter you.

The amplification in this verse instructs you to do "more than enough" as you serve the Lord. Commit everything to doing what God has called you to do. A subsequent amplification in this verse says that your labor for the Lord "is never wasted." You cannot spend your time more profitably than to be totally committed to carrying out God's assignment for your life.

Many people waste their lives. They focus completely on the pursuit of personal goals. They have no understanding of the eternal significance of completing God's assignment for their lives. God instructs you to follow the example of the Macedonians in the following verse of Scripture. "…first they gave themselves to the Lord and to us [as His agents] by the will of God [entirely disregarding their personal interests, they gave as much as they possibly could, having put themselves at our disposal to be directed by the will of God]" (II Corinthians 8:5)

Give yourself completely to the Lord. Disregard the pursuit of personal interests as you focus on doing what God has called you to do with your life. Give your all to God every day. Put yourself completely at God's disposal by turning away from preoccupation with personal desires to focus on carrying out the will of God.

John Wesley was an 18th century British theologian who founded the Methodist church. He traveled on horseback throughout Great Britain often preaching two or three times a day. John Wesley once said, "Do all the good you can by all the means you can, in all the ways you can, in all the places you can, to all the people you can for as long as you can."

John Wesley emphasized total commitment to serving God and to serving other people. Make the quality decision to devote your life to successfully completing the assignment God has given to you. What could possibly be more important?

You saw in Ephesians 2:10 in Chapter 1 and again in this chapter that you have access to the perfect will of God when you receive Jesus Christ as your Savior. Look at the remainder of your life from an eternal perspective. "…You have made my days as [short as] handbreadths, and my lifetime is as nothing in Your sight. Truly every man at his best is merely a breath!" (Psalm 39:5)

The length of the 70, 80 or 90 years that most people expect to live on earth is completely insignificant compared to the equivalent of the endless trillions of years of eternity where you will live in heaven with Jesus Christ. Devote the relatively short period of your remaining years on earth to continually seeking, finding and carrying out God's will for your life.

This chapter has been devoted to one word – *commitment.* If the great scriptural truths in the first 14 chapters of this book have motivated you deeply to seek, find and successfully complete God's assignment for your life, now is the time to commit totally to this magnificent goal. The remainder of this book will be devoted to Scripture that will explain exactly what God instructs you to do as you completely commit to carrying out His assignment for your life.

Chapter 16

God Will Bring You Through
Every Problem

When you are in the center of God's will for your life, you can be certain that God is with you every step of the way. He will be with you through all adversity if you have absolute faith in Him and if you persevere for as long as He requires you to persevere. "We are assured and know that [God being a partner in their labor] all things work together and are [fitting into a plan] for good to and for those who love God and are called according to [His] design and purpose." (Romans 8:28)

Please note the words "God being a partner in their labor" in the amplification of this verse. If God is a *partner* in what you are doing, how can you possibly fail? God is your partner when you are in the center of His will for your life. This verse assures you that everything *will* work together for good *if* you love God and you are doing what He has called you to do.

If you love God with all of your heart (see Matthew 22:37-38) and you are completely committed to carrying out His assignment for your life, you can be absolutely certain that

God ultimately will cause everything to work out for good. "…with God nothing is ever impossible…" (Luke 1:37)

These words that an angel spoke to the virgin Mary many years ago apply to your life today if you are in the center of God's will for your life. Absolutely refuse to give up, no matter how difficult any problems you face might seem. You have just seen that God is your partner when you are in His will. God is not concerned in the least with His ability to solve whatever problems you face. If you are certain that you are in the center of God's will for your life, do your very best to look at every challenge you face from God's perspective. Jesus said, "…With men [it is] impossible, but not with God; for all things are possible with God." (Mark 10:27)

All things are possible for God (see I Corinthians 1:8-9, II Corinthians 3:5 and 4:7 and Philippians 2:13). "Alas, Lord God! Behold, You have made the heavens and the earth by Your great power and by Your outstretched arm! There is nothing too hard or too wonderful for You" (Jeremiah 32:17)

The Bible repeatedly emphasizes that nothing is impossible for God Who created heaven and earth. Nothing is impossible for you if you are doing what God has called you to do. Have absolute faith that God is with you and that He will bring you safely through to successfully complete His assignment for your life.

If you have read the book of Job, you know that Job experienced significant adversity in his life. Job was certain that God was with him. He knew that nothing could stop God. "…Job said to the Lord, I know that You can do all things, and that no thought or purpose of Yours can be restrained or thwarted." (Job 42:1-2)

God can do *all* things. *Nothing* can stop Him. "…if this doctrine or purpose or undertaking or movement is of human origin, it will fail (be overthrown and come to nothing);

but if it is of God, you will not be able to stop or overthrow or destroy them…" (Acts 5:38-39)

If what you are doing is part of your personal goals for your life, you definitely can fail. However, if you are doing what God has called you to do, *nothing* will be able to stop you. You cannot fail because God never fails. All that God asks is for you to have absolute faith in Him and the reliability of these promises.

Persevere in your faith in God, absolutely refusing to give up. Do not block God through doubt and unbelief (see Mark 6:1-6). "…thanks be to God, Who in Christ always leads us in triumph [as trophies of Christ's victory]…" (II Corinthians 2:14)

When we studied Ephesians 2:10 in Chapter 1 and again in the last chapter, you saw that you were recreated in Jesus Christ to do the good works that God has planned for you. If you are in the center of God's will, the supernatural victory that Jesus Christ won when He rose from the dead applies to you.

Please note the word "always" in this verse. If you know that you are doing what God has called you to do, do not give up. If you are carrying out God's plan for your life, nothing can stop you because nothing can stop God. "…what He wants to do, that He does." (Job 23:13)

This chapter is filled with Scripture assuring you that nothing can stop God and that nothing can stop you if you are in the center of God's will. God will never fail you. "…He [God] Himself has said, I will not in any way fail you nor give you up nor leave you without support. [I will] not, [I will] not, [I will] not in any degree leave you helpless nor forsake nor let [you] down (relax My hold on you)! [Assuredly not!]" (Hebrews 13:5)

The words "I will not" are used four times in this verse and the amplification. Your Father wants you to be absolutely certain that He will *never* fail you, leave you or forsake you. Trust Him completely. Persevere with unwavering faith that He will guide you to successfully complete His assignment for your life. "...those who are ill-treated and suffer in accordance with God's will must do right and commit their souls [in charge as a deposit] to the One Who created [them] and will never fail [them]." (I Peter 4:19)

Commit everything to God if you are facing severe severity and you know that you are in God's will. The same God Who created you will never fail you or let you down. "The Lord will fight for you, and you shall hold your peace and remain at rest." (Exodus 14:14)

God repeatedly promises that He will fight your battles for you (see Deuteronomy 20:1-4 and II Chronicles 20:15 and 32:8). "Trust in, lean on, rely on, and have confidence in Him at all times..." (Psalm 62:8)

How often does God instruct you to trust Him, to lean on Him, to rely on Him and to have confidence in Him? He instructs you to trust Him *at all times*. If you are doing what God has called you to do, you cannot fail because God cannot fail.

This chapter is filled with awesome promises from God assuring you that He will bring you safely through any and all problems you face when you are in the center of His will for your life. If you know that you are in the center of God's will, meditate day and night on these supernatural promises from God when you face adversity (see Chapter 7). Absolutely refuse to give up.

If you are doing what God has called you to do, you can be certain that you *will* face many obstacles along the way. Do not allow these obstacles to defeat you. No matter what adversity you face, God *will* bring you safely through if you trust Him completely.

God never loses. He wins every time. You have nothing to fear. Refuse to give in to fear. The *only* way that you can be defeated when you are in the center of God's will is if you give up because your faith and perseverance are not strong enough. Some people give up *just before* God would have brought them safely through if they had persevered.

Chapter 17

Pray Continually for God's Will for Your Life

Prayer is important in two areas pertaining to God's assignment for your life. If you do not know God's plan, pray continually with unwavering faith until God reveals His plan to you. If you do know what God's plan is, pray continually for guidance to successfully complete what God has called you to do. "…we also, from the day we heard of it, have not ceased to pray and make [special] request for you, [asking] that you may be filled with the full (deep and clear) knowledge of His will…" (Colossians 1:9)

Paul and Timothy prayed that each member of a church in Colossae would be filled with the full knowledge of God's will for his or her life. This same principle applies to praying to be filled with the full knowledge of God's specific plan for your life.

Your Father does not want you to have a vague and indefinite concept of His will. He wants each of His children to be filled with "full, deep and clear knowledge" of exactly what He has called him or her to do. Do not hesitate to pray often regarding God's assignment for your life. "…You do not have, because you do not ask." (James 4:2)

Many people do not receive what they desire from God because they do not pray to Him. If you are praying in regard to God's will for your life, you can be absolutely certain that your Father hears your prayer. "…this is the confidence (the assurance, the privilege of boldness) which we have in Him: [we are sure] that if we ask anything (make any request) according to His will (in agreement with His own plan), He listens to and hears us." (I John 5:14)

There is no question that God *hears* each and every prayer request that you make in regard to His will for your life. In addition to assuring you that He hears every prayer, your Father promises to answer every prayer that is in agreement with His will. "And if (since) we [positively] know that He listens to us in whatever we ask, we also know [with settled and absolute knowledge] that we have [granted us as our present possessions] the requests made of Him." (I John 5:15)

The word "know" is used twice in this verse. Your Father wants you to be absolutely certain that He *listens* to every prayer regarding His will for your life and that He will *answer* each of those prayers.

The words "present possessions" in the amplification of this verse are very important. God promises to answer every prayer in regard to His will for your life immediately in the spiritual realm. This is why the words "present possessions" are used in this promise.

God often requires patience and perseverance to bring into manifestation the answer to prayer in the natural realm that He already has given to you in the spiritual realm. Pray with absolute faith that God will answer every prayer that you bring to Him regarding His plan for your life. Jesus Christ said, "…whatever you ask for in prayer, having faith and [really] believing, you will receive." (Matthew 21:22)

Jesus has promised that God will answer every prayer you bring to Him with deep, strong and unwavering faith that He hears your prayer and that He will answer. Pray fervently and often in regard to God's assignment for your life. "...The earnest (heartfelt, continued) prayer of a righteous man makes tremendous power available [dynamic in its working]." (James 5:16)

This verse of Scripture instructs you to pray earnestly – to pray with deep commitment. The amplification instructs you to pray continually from your heart. If you obey these specific instructions when you pray, your prayer will release the supernatural power of God to accomplish His plan for your life.

God often requires persevering prayers of faith to bring His answer into manifestation in the natural realm. Jesus said, "...I say to you, Ask and keep on asking and it shall be given you; seek and keep on seeking and you shall find; knock and keep on knocking and the door shall be opened to you. For everyone who asks and keeps on asking receives; and he who seeks and keeps on seeking finds; and to him who knocks and keeps on knocking, the door shall be opened." (Luke 11:9-10)

The words "keep on" and "keeps on" are used *six times* in this passage of Scripture. We often say that God emphasizes through repetition. Your Father instructs you to *persevere* in your prayers for Him to guide you and to anoint you to successfully complete His assignment for your life.

If you keep on asking, God promises to respond. If you keep on seeking, you will find what you seek. If you keep on knocking, God will open the door.

The word "everyone" in verse 10 includes you. Persevere in your prayers pertaining to finding and carrying out God's assignment for your life. This book is filled with promises from God regarding His will for your life. Base your prayers on these specific promises. God will reveal every aspect of His plan for your life if you pray consistently to Him with unwavering faith. Have absolute faith that your Father will reveal every detail regarding His plan in His way and in His good timing.

We will devote the remainder of this chapter to studying God's promises to strengthen you to carry out His assignment for your life. God said, "...I am your God. I will strengthen and harden you to difficulties, yes, I will help you; yes, I will hold you up and retain you with My [victorious] right hand of rightness and justice." (Isaiah 41:10)

In the last chapter we studied several verses of Scripture pertaining to what God promises when you face adversity and you are in the center of His will for your life. You saw that nothing is impossible for God. God *will* strengthen you when you face difficult problems as you carry out His assignment for your life. God promises to help you. Receive by faith the supernatural strength that He promises to give you. "...be strong in the Lord [be empowered through your union with Him]; draw your strength from Him [that strength which His boundless might provides]." (Ephesians 6:10)

If you consistently stay close to God, you will draw supernatural strength from Him. "He gives power to the faint and weary, and to him who has no might He increases strength [causing it to multiply and making it to abound]." (Isaiah 40:29)

Are you faint and weary? Trust God to give you the strength, power and ability that you require to carry out His assignment. When you have "no might" in your human strength and ability, trust your Father completely to increase your strength to do what He has called you to do. God said, "...My strength and power are made perfect (fulfilled and completed) and show themselves most effective in [your] weakness...." (II Corinthians 12:9)

Receive by faith the supernatural strength and power that God promises to give you. Refuse to focus on any human weakness that you have. Rejoice in your certainty that the supernatural strength of God *is* available to enable you to carry out His assignment for your life.

Refuse to complain about any problems you face (see Exodus 1:8, Numbers 11:1 and Philippians 2:14). Rejoice because you are certain that God will supernaturally strengthen you to do what He has called you to do. "...I am well pleased and take pleasure in infirmities, insults, hardships, persecutions, perplexities and distresses; for when I am weak [in human strength], then am I [truly] strong (able, powerful in divine strength)." (II Corinthians 12:10)

We often emphasize that God's ways are very different and very much higher than the ways of human beings (see Isaiah 55:8-9). Your Father actually instructs you to *take pleasure in* the adversity you encounter when you are doing your best to carry out His assignment. Why wouldn't you rejoice if you are absolutely certain that God will give you His supernatural strength? "I have strength for all things in Christ Who empowers me [I am ready for anything and equal to anything through Him Who infuses inner strength into me; I am self-sufficient in Christ's sufficiency]." (Philippians 4:13)

Philippians 4:13 is my favorite verse of Scripture. I have meditated on this supernatural promise thousands of times during the past 39 years. I repeatedly open my mouth to speak this great spiritual truth as I meditate on Philippians 4:13. *My ears* often hear *my mouth* boldly speaking this promise from God. My faith in this promise from God increases steadily as a result (see Romans 10:17). No matter what problem I face, I am certain that Jesus Christ will strengthen me.

The amplification in this verse assures you that you are ready for *anything* and equal to *anything* through the strength that will come to you from within yourself. You saw in Chapter 10 that the victorious Jesus Christ is omnipresent. Jesus sits on a throne in heaven next to God. He also lives in your heart and in the heart of every person who has received Him as his or her Savior.

Trust Jesus completely to "infuse inner strength into you." God has supernaturally provided all of the strength, power and ability that you will need to carry out His assignment for your life. Trust Him completely. Absolutely refuse to give up.

Chapter 18

Patience, Perseverance and God's Will for Your Life

Your faith in God will be challenged many times when you are striving to carry out God's assignment for your life. Your Father often will require great patience and perseverance to do what He has called you to do. "Do not, therefore, fling away your fearless confidence, for it carries a great and glorious compensation of reward. For you have need of steadfast patience and endurance, so that you may perform and fully accomplish the will of God, and thus receive and carry away [and enjoy to the full] what is promised." (Hebrews 10:35-36)

If you have studied and meditated on the many promises in this book pertaining to God's will, you should have "fearless confidence" that God will do in you, through you and for you exactly what He has called you to do. This passage of Scripture specifically refers to fully accomplishing God's will for your life.

Your Father wants you to have absolute confidence that He does have a specific plan for your life. He wants you to be certain that He will reward you abundantly if you are patient and persevering in your faith as you move forward to accomplish His assignment for your life. "…let us run with patient endurance and steady and active persistence the appointed course of the race that is set before us, looking away [from all that will distract] to Jesus, Who is the Leader and the Source of our faith [giving the first incentive for our belief] and is also its Finisher [bringing it to maturity and perfection]…" (Hebrews 12:1-2)

The words "the appointed course of the race that is set before us" in Hebrews 12:1 refer to God's specific plan for your life. Once again your Father explains that patience and perseverance will be required to successfully complete His assignment for your life in Christ Jesus.

Focus continually on the victorious Jesus Christ Who makes His permanent home in your heart (see II Corinthians 13:5, Galatians 2:20 and Ephesians 3:17). Jesus is your Leader. He is the Source of your faith. He is the Finisher. Trust Jesus completely to strengthen you to do whatever God has called you to do.

The apostle Paul was totally dedicated to completing God's assignment for his life. Paul said, "…one thing I do [it is my one aspiration]: forgetting what lies behind and straining forward to what lies ahead, I press on toward the goal to win the [supreme and heavenly] prize to which God in Christ Jesus is calling us upward." (Philippians 3:13-14)

Paul was single-minded. He focused on one thing above all else – to forget anything in the past as he moved steadily forward to accomplish the specific assignment that God gave him. Please note the words "I press on toward the goal" in verse 14. Paul knew what he was called to do. He continually persevered with faith. "Let your eyes look right on [with fixed purpose], and let your gaze be straight before you." (Proverbs 4:25)

The words "with fixed purpose" in the amplification of this verse instruct you to be very specific in accomplishing your goal. Do not turn to the right. Do not turn to the left. Keep moving straight ahead to accomplish God's assignment for your life. We are instructed to "...hold fast and firm to the end our joyful and exultant confidence and sense of triumph in our hope [in Christ]." (Hebrews 3:6)

You are instructed to hold firmly to your absolute certainty that Jesus Christ has won a victory over every problem you face. Follow the example of the apostle Paul who said, "...the Holy Spirit clearly and emphatically affirms to me in city after city that imprisonment and suffering await me. But none of these things move me; neither do I esteem my life dear to myself, if only I may finish my course with joy and the ministry which I have obtained from [which was entrusted to me by] the Lord Jesus, faithfully to attest to the good news (Gospel) of God's grace (His unmerited favor, spiritual blessing, and mercy)." (Acts 20:23-24)

Paul was totally dedicated to carrying out God's plan for his life. He knew that he repeatedly would face imprisonment and suffering, but he did not allow contemplation of this severe adversity to move him. Paul focused totally, completely and absolutely on completing the assignment that Jesus Christ had given to him.

Paul emphasized the importance of completing this assignment *with joy*. Refuse to be discouraged by the severity of any problems you face in carrying out God's will. "...be not grieved and depressed, for the joy of the Lord is your strength and stronghold." (Nehemiah 8:10)

God instructs you not to be grieved and depressed. You have seen that God is your partner when you pursue His plan for your life (see Romans 8:28). He will provide the supernatural strength that you need to persevere through adversity. Follow the example of the psalmist who said, "I will cry to God Most High, Who performs on my behalf and rewards me [Who brings to pass His purposes for me and surely completes them]!" (Psalm 57:2)

The amplification in this verse refers specifically to God's plan for your life. Pray to your Father with absolute certainty that He will "perform on your behalf." You saw in Chapter 12 that God has a specific time for everything (see Ecclesiastes 3:1). "...the vision is yet for an appointed time and it hastens to the end [fulfillment]; it will not deceive or disappoint. Though it tarry, wait [earnestly] for it, because it will surely come; it will not be behindhand on its appointed day." (Habakkuk 2:3)

God may give you a clear vision of His plan for your life. God often gives a vision to His children for an appointed time. God will not disappoint you if you persevere patiently, knowing that He will do in you, through you and for you what He has called you to do. "...let us not lose heart and grow weary and faint in acting nobly and doing right, for in due time and at the appointed season we shall reap, if we do not loosen and relax our courage and faint." (Galatians 6:9)

Please note the words "at the appointed season" in this verse. Do not give up. Trust God's timing just as you trust Him in other areas. The Bible speaks of "...those who through faith (by their leaning of the entire personality on God in Christ in absolute trust and confidence in His power, wisdom, and goodness) and by practice of patient endurance and waiting are [now] inheriting the promises." (Hebrews 6:12)

This verse explains that you often will be required to add patient endurance to your faith to receive manifestation of God's promises. We like the definition of faith in the amplification of this verse. Faith is described as the "leaning of the entire personality on God in Christ in absolute trust and confidence in His power, wisdom, and goodness." God is looking for *this* kind of faith from you as you move steadily forward to successfully complete His assignment for your life. Trust God's timing completely just as the psalmist David did when he said, "My times are in Your hands..." (Psalm 31:15)

God's timing is perfect. God is never late, even though He may seem to be late. Do not make the mistake of rushing ahead of God. "...to be overhasty is to sin and miss the mark." (Proverbs 19:2)

You sin when you try to make things happen instead of waiting on God. Refuse to be impatient. Move steadily forward to do what God has called you to do. "Be still and rest in the Lord; wait for Him and patiently lean yourself upon Him..." (Psalm 37:7)

Your Father instructs you to be still, quiet and calm as you rest in Him. I can tell you from many years of personal experience that successfully doing what God calls us to do often requires significant patience and perseverance. Carrying out God's assignment is a marathon, not a sprint.

You can be certain that your faith in God will be challenged on many occasions if you sincerely pursue His assignment for your life. Keep moving forward. Refuse to give up. Do not waver in your faith that God *will* bring you to the successful completion of His assignment for your life in His way and in His perfect timing.

Jesus Christ has given you victory over every obstacle you will ever face. No matter what problems you face, Jesus has overcome these problems. He said, "I have told you these things, so that in Me you may have [perfect] peace and confidence. In the world you have tribulation and trials and distress and frustration; but be of good cheer [take courage; be confident, certain, undaunted]! For I have overcome the world. [I have deprived it of power to harm you and have conquered it for you.]" (John 16:33)

Expect to face "tribulation and trials and distress and frustration" as you pursue God's will. What does Jesus instruct you to do? Instead of giving in to adversity, Jesus instructs you to "be of good cheer." Absolutely refuse to give up. Identify with the total, complete and absolute victory that Jesus won when He rose from the dead.

Conclusion

You learned in Chapter 1 that God has a specific plan for the life of every person He created. God has a specific and definite plan for *your* life. What could possibly be more important than for you to complete the assignment that God had for you when He created you in your mother's womb? This book is filled with specific scriptural instructions that explain exactly what God instructs you to do to seek, find and carry out His will for your life.

In the Introduction we recommended that you highlight or underline key scriptural principles that were important to you. If you did this, you now can go back and meditate on this Scripture. You saw in Chapter 7 the importance of meditating day and night on God's Word. *Immerse* yourself in Scripture pertaining to God's assignment for your life.

We pray that this book will help you to find and complete God's assignment for your life. You undoubtedly have many Christians in your sphere of influence who have not yet found God's plan for their lives. Please pray about sharing a copy of this book to help these people to seek, find and carry out God's assignment for their lives.

Take advantage of the quantity discounts that we offer. From the beginning God has instructed us to give our readers similar discounts to the ones that bookstores receive when they buy books in quantity. The order form at the back of this book explains these discounts. Please pray about helping other Christians to find God's assignment for their lives.

If this book has helped you, would you share your testimony with us so that we can share with others what you have learned about God's plan for your life? We normally need three to four paragraphs in a testimony so that we can consolidate this information into one solid paragraph for our newsletter and our website. Your comments will encourage many people, including pastors and leaders in Third World countries and inmates in prisons and jails who receive our books free of charge.

Please send any comments to lamplightmin@yahoo.com. You can call 1-800-540-1597 and leave a message for Judy. You also can mail your comments to PO Box 1307, Dunedin, FL 34697.

We invite you to visit our website: www.lamplight.net. You will find many comments from people who have been helped by our books. You also will find a section on biblical health as well as recipes that Judy adds each month to bless you. We are in good health at ages 81 and 74. I know that I would not be alive today if it were not for Judy's knowledge and wisdom regarding health and her amazing recipes.

You can keep in touch with us at facebook.com/jackandjudylamplight and at twitter.com/lamplightmin. You can follow our blog at lamplightmin.wordpress.com You can receive frequent updates on our latest books.

We have been blessed to share with you the results of many hours of effort that we have invested to help you find God's will for your life. We would be so pleased to hear from you. Blessed to be a blessing. (Genesis 12:1-3)

Jack and Judy

Appendix

Trusting in Jesus Christ as Your Savior

This book is filled with instructions and promises from God. However, if you have not received Jesus Christ as your Savior, you *cannot understand* the scriptural truths that are contained in this book. "...the mind of the flesh [with its carnal thoughts and purposes] is hostile to God, for it does not submit itself to God's Law; indeed it cannot." (Romans 8:7)

Please notice the word "cannot" in this verse of Scripture. If Jesus is not your Savior, you cannot understand and obey God's instructions.

Many people who have not received Jesus Christ as their Savior are not open to the specific instructions that God has given to us in the Bible. "...the natural, nonspiritual man does not accept or welcome or admit into his heart the gifts and teachings and revelations of the Spirit of God, for they are folly (meaningless nonsense) to him; and he is incapable of knowing them [of progressively recognizing, understanding, and becoming better acquainted with them] because they are spiritually discerned and estimated and appreciated." (I Corinthians 2:14)

The words "does not accept or welcome or admit into his heart the gifts and teachings and revelations of the Spirit of God" in this verse of Scripture are very important. Some people are strongly opposed to the Bible and what it teaches. They look at Scripture references from the Bible as "meaningless nonsense." These people are incapable of learning great scriptural truths from God until and unless they receive Jesus Christ as their Savior.

At the close of this Appendix we will explain exactly what God instructs you to do to receive Jesus Christ as your Savior. If and when you make this decision, the glorious supernatural truths of the Bible will open up to you. Jesus said, "…To you it has been given to know the secrets and mysteries of the kingdom of heaven, but to them it has not been given." (Matthew 13:11)

Jesus was speaking to *you* when He said that you can "know the secrets and mysteries of the kingdom of heaven." Do not miss out on the glorious privilege that is available to every believer to know and understand the ways of God.

A spiritual veil blocks all unbelievers from understanding the things of God. "…even if our Gospel (the glad tidings) also be hidden (obscured and covered up with a veil that hinders the knowledge of God), it is hidden [only] to those who are perishing and obscured [only] to those who are spiritually dying and veiled [only] to those who are lost." (II Corinthians 4:3)

When and if you receive Jesus Christ as your Savior, this spiritual veil is pulled aside. "…whenever a person turns [in repentance] to the Lord, the veil is stripped off and taken away." (II Corinthians 3:16)

If you obey the scriptural instructions at the end of this Appendix, Jesus Christ will become your Savior. Everything in your life will become fresh and new. "…if any person is [ingrafted] in Christ (the Messiah) he is a new creation (a new creature altogether); the old [previous moral and spiritual condition] has passed away. Behold, the fresh and new has come!" (II Corinthians 5:17)

Instead of being opposed to the teachings of the holy Bible, you will be completely open to these teachings. You will have a hunger and thirst to continually learn more supernatural truths from the Word of God. "…I endorse and delight in the Law of God in my inmost self [with my new nature]." (Romans 7:22)

Every person who has not received Jesus Christ as his or her Savior is a sinner who is doomed to live throughout eternity in the horror of hell. God has made it possible for *you* to escape this terrible eternal penalty. "…God so greatly loved and dearly prized the world that He [even] gave up His only begotten (unique) Son, so that whoever believes in (trusts in, clings to, relies on) Him shall not perish (come to destruction, be lost) but have eternal (everlasting) life." (John 3:16)

God knew that everyone who lived on earth after Adam and Eve would be a sinner because of the sins of Adam and Eve (see Romans 3:10-12). He sent His only Son to take upon Himself the sins of the world as He died a horrible death by crucifixion. If you believe that Jesus Christ paid the full price for *your* sins and if you trust Him completely for your eternal salvation, you will live with Him eternally in the glory of heaven.

There is only *one* way for you to live eternally in heaven after you die – that is to receive eternal salvation through Jesus Christ. "Jesus said to him, I am the Way and the Truth and the Life; no one comes to the Father except by (through) Me." (John 14:6)

If you trust in anyone or anything except Jesus Christ for your eternal salvation, you will not live eternally in heaven. If you are reading these truths about living eternally in heaven because of the price that Jesus Christ has paid for you, you can be certain that the same God Who created you actually is drawing you to come to Jesus Christ for eternal salvation. Jesus said, "No one is able to come to Me unless the Father Who sent Me attracts and draws him and gives him the desire to come to Me…" (John 6:44)

Are you interested in these spiritual truths about where you will live throughout eternity? If you are, you can be certain that the same awesome God Who created you is drawing *you* to Jesus Christ at this very moment.

Heaven is a glorious place. Everyone in heaven is completely healthy and very happy. "God will wipe away every tear from their eyes; and death shall be no more, neither shall there be anguish (sorrow and mourning) nor grief nor pain any more, for the old conditions and the former order of things have passed away." (Revelation 21:4)

All of the problems of earth will disappear when you arrive in heaven. No one in heaven dies. No one in heaven is sad. No one in heaven cries. No one in heaven suffers from pain.

You *will* live throughout eternity in one place or another after you die. If you do not receive Jesus Christ as your Savior, you will live eternally in hell. People in hell will experience continual torment throughout eternity. "…the smoke of their torment ascends forever and ever; and they have no respite (no pause, no intermission, no rest, no peace) day or night…" (Revelation 14:11)

Everyone in heaven is filled with joy. Everyone in hell is miserable. Jesus described what hell would be like when He said, "...there will be weeping and wailing and grinding of teeth. (Matthew 13:42)

Throughout eternity the inhabitants of hell will weep and wail. They will grind their teeth in anguish. Can you imagine living this way for the endless trillions of years of eternity? This is exactly what will happen if you *reject* the supreme sacrifice that Jesus Christ made to pay the full price for your sins.

How do you receive eternal salvation through Jesus Christ? "...if you acknowledge and confess with your lips that Jesus is Lord and in your heart believe (adhere to, trust in, and rely on the truth) that God raised Him from the dead, you will be saved. For with the heart a person believes (adheres to, trusts in, and relies on Christ) and so is justified (declared righteous, acceptable to God), and with the mouth he confesses (declares openly and speaks out freely his faith) and confirms [his] salvation." (Romans 10:9-10)

Repent of your sins. You must *believe in your heart* (not just think in your mind) that Jesus Christ paid the full price for all of your sins when He was crucified. You must believe that God actually raised Jesus from the dead. You must open your mouth and *speak* this truth that you believe in your heart. If you believe in your heart that Jesus Christ died and rose again from the dead and that the price for your sins has been paid for and you tell others that you believe this great spiritual truth, you *have* been saved. You *will* live eternally in heaven.

If Jesus Christ was not your Savior when you began to read this book, we pray that He is your Savior now. Your life will change immensely. You will never be the same again. Every aspect of your life will be gloriously new.

If you have become a child of God by receiving eternal salvation through Jesus Christ, please let us know by contacting us at lamplightmin@yahoo.com, 1-800-540-1497 or PO Box 1307, Dunedin, FL 34697. We would like to pray for you and welcome you as our new Christian brother or sister. We love you and bless you in the name of our Lord Jesus Christ.

We would be so pleased to hear from you. If you are already a believer, we would be pleased to hear from you as well. We invite you to visit our website at www.lamplight.net. Please let us know if this book or one or more of our other publications has made a difference in our life. Please give us your comments so that we can share these comments in our newsletters and on our website to encourage other people.

Study Guide

What Did You Learn From This Book?

The questions in this Study Guide are carefully arranged to show you how much you have learned about God's plan for your life. This Study Guide is not intended to be an academic test. The sole purpose of the following questions is to help you increase your practical knowledge pertaining to God's plan for your life.

Page Reference

1. What did the psalmist David say about the omniscience of God? What minute details does God know about your life? (Psalm 139:1-4) 14

2. When did God plan all of the days of the life of David? (Psalm 139:16) 15

3. When did God decide that Jeremiah would be a prophet to the nations? (Jeremiah 1:5).................... 15

4. If God had a specific plan for the lives of David and Jeremiah before they were born, why can you believe that God had a specific plan for your life before He created you? (Acts 10:34 and Matthew 10:30) 15-16

A Few Words About Lamplight Ministries

Lamplight Ministries, Inc. originally began in 1983 as Lamplight Publications. After ten years as a publishing firm with a goal of selling Christian books, Lamplight Ministries was established in 1993. Jack and Judy Hartman founded Lamplight Ministries with a mission of continuing to sell their publications and also to *give* large numbers of these publications free of charge to needy people all over the world.

Lamplight Ministries was created to allow people who have been blessed by our publications to share in financing the translation, printing and distribution of our books into other languages and also to distribute our publications free of charge to inmates in jails and prisons. Over the years many partners of Lamplight Ministries have shared Jack and Judy's vision. Thousands of people in jails and prisons and in Third World countries have received our publications free of charge.

Our books and Scripture Meditation Cards have been translated into eleven foreign languages – Armenian, Danish, Greek, Hebrew, German, Korean, Norwegian, Portuguese, Russian, Spanish and the Tamil dialect in India. The translations in these languages are not available from Lamplight Ministries in the United States. These translations can only be obtained in the countries where we have given permission for them to be published.

The pastors of many churches in Third World countries have written to say that they consistently preach sermons in their churches based on the scriptural contents of our publications. We believe that people in several churches in many different countries consistently hear sermons that are based on the scriptural contents of our publications. Praise the Lord!

Jack Hartman was the sole author of twelve Christian books. After co-authoring one book with Judy, Jack and Judy co-authored ten sets of Scripture Meditation Cards. Judy has been the co-author of every subsequent book. Jack and Judy currently are working on other books that they believe the Lord is leading them to write as co-authors.

We invite you to request our newsletters to stay in touch with us, to learn of our latest publications and to read comments from people all over the world. Please write, fax, call or email us. You are very special to us. We love you and thank God for you. Our heart is to take the gospel to the world and for our books to be available in every known language. Hallelujah!

Lamplight Ministries, Inc.,

PO Box 1307 - Dunedin, Florida, 34697. USA

Phone: 1-800-540-1597 • Fax: 1-727-784-2980

website: lamplight.net • email: lamplightmin@yahoo.com

facebook.com/jackandjudylamplight

twitter.com/lamplightmin

blog: lamplightmin.wordpress.com

Enthusiastic Comments from Readers of Our Publications

The following are just a few of the many comments we have received from people in more than 60 countries pertaining to our publications. For additional comments, see our website: lamplight.net.

Trust God for Your Finances

There are more than 150,000 copies of *Trust God for Your Finances* in print. This book has been translated into seven foreign languages.

- "I have translated *Trust God for Your Finances* into Thai. I intended to make about 50 or 60 photocopies of this translation to distribute among friends. My pastor asked for 700 copies to distribute at the special yearly conference for pastors. My immediate thought was that I could not do this, but he urged me to pray and try my best. Surprisingly, it worked out. Thank God. More than 1,000 people attended the conference. Seven hundred copies were distributed to only the pastors, elders and deacons who really wanted the book. After the conference, we had so many calls that another 2,000 copies were printed. Thank you, Mr. Hartman, for this book which is helping so many Thai Christians." (Thailand)
- "I bought your book, *Trust God for Your Finances,* at a church I was attending in Virginia in the 1980s. This book

transformed my life. It was all Bible-based and solid in every way. I married a Bulgarian pastor who started the church here during Communism and the underground church. We have pastored together for 22 years. I gave your book to my husband and he consumed it. He kept it near his Bible all the time. God has raised him up to be influential in this nation. He has written a book titled *The Covenant of Provision* dealing with finances. Your book helped him so much to form his ideas about the rightful use of money. This book has influenced my husband more than almost any other book. It was so timely and needed coming out of a Communist society. Thank you so much for this book." (Bulgaria)

- "Today we had a ministry partner join us for lunch. He said that the book, *Trust God for Your Finances*, that we had translated into Hebrew was the most powerful book he had ever read on the subject. I shared with him the wonderful story of how you shared the book with us and how many Israelis have been enlightened in that area as a result of reading the book. You both are a blessing and a treasure in God's kingdom." (Israel)

God's Instructions for Growing Older
- "I am a 63-year-old businesswoman from Thailand. Like most women around the world, I do not like growing old. When I received a copy of your book, *God's Instructions For Growing Older*, I read straight from the first page to the last in two days. Your book gives me the assurance of how to grow older without fear, anxiety, and worry. I will live the rest of my life in peace and joy for I now know that if we keep God in first place at all times, the final years of our lives will be meaningful, productive, and fulfilling. Thank you, Mr. and Mrs. Hartman, for the priceless gift of your book. May God bless you and your team always." (Thailand)

- "I have never read a book like *God's Instructions for Growing Older*. Finally a book has been written that teaches how to finish our course in life as a Christian. Your chapter on Scripture meditation is pure gold. This book is a road map to direct us in the way the Lord intends for us to grow older. Thank you so much for this special book." (Florida)
- "Thank you for your new book, *God's Instructions for Growing Older.* I love this book. I read a little bit every day so that I can be an encourager to my older friends and to myself. We so need God's knowledge during the final years of our lives. I have started my gift list to share this book with others." (Texas)

You Can Hear the Voice of God

- "Many years of my life I scoffed at Christians. I looked at them as holy rollers. When I was incarcerated, I experienced pain as I have never felt in my life. A darkness and loneliness like I have never experienced before came upon me. A friend here gave me your book, *You Can Hear the Voice of God.* If there ever was a time when I needed to hear from God, it is now. My wife was desperately ill at the very point of death when I started reading your book. I now know that God has been trying to talk to me all of my life, but I didn't know how to listen to His voice. NOW I CAN HEAR THE VOICE OF GOD. In a splendid and simple way you actually taught me how to hear the voice of God Almighty. How can I ever thank you? Thank you for writing this book. It will impact hundreds of thousands, I am sure." (Florida)
- "Thank you for sending me a copy of *You Can Hear the Voice of God.* This book is so good. On the first day of having this book in my hands, I read continually. I finished five chapters. My wife was invited to teach at a meeting of pastors' wives. The women were excited because of

this teaching. I would like to translate this book into Benba, one of the largest spoken languages on the copper belt and some provinces of Zambia. Would you give me permission to translate this book? I know that the Holy Spirit has inspired me to do so." (Permission was granted.) (Zambia)

- "Thank you for the box of books that you sent to a pastor who is a friend of mine. He gave me a copy of your book *You Can Hear The Voice of God.* This book is a spiritual manual for the serious Christian. I thank God for Jack and Judy Hartman. This book is helping me to draw closer to my Maker. I now realize that God has been talking to me daily but I did not hear Him. This book is a real blessing to the body of Christ." (Ghana)

Effective Prayer
- "I thank God for your book titled *Effective Prayer.* This book came to me at the right time. Since reading this book, God has done great wonders in my life and ministry. Our whole church is being affected by what we have learned about the power of prayer. I have read many books on prayer, but this one is unique. I no longer pray amiss. My prayer life has become much more effective. Your book has helped me to persevere in prayer much longer than before. This is a great book. I love it. I treasure this book. I do not know how to thank you. I pray that God will bless you both with long life and that you will enjoy the fruit of your labour." (Zambia)
- "Your book *Effective Prayer* is a great blessing to me. After reading this book I have so much more understanding about prayer. It is very easy to learn from all that you are teaching and all of the Scriptures in it. I now understand much more about the significance of prayer in my daily life, why I should pray and how to pray. You have enlightened my mind. I know that my

loving Father wants me to pray all the time. I have learned to pray God's answer instead of focusing on the problem. This book is very vital to my daily life. I am so thankful to both of you for another great book for people who need answers. Thank you so much for the great understanding that I found in this book." (the Philippines)

- "I have been studying your book *Effective Prayer.* This book has inspired me to do a lot more praying. Praying to God is such a privilege. To know that God is just waiting for me to come and talk with Him is tremendous. The way you brought out the gift of being baptized in the Holy Spirit and praying in tongues will make it easier for people to receive this much-needed gift in their lives. Our pastor is using your book to teach on prayer. I have given copies of this book to many people in our church. I gave one to another pastor in our town. I love you both in the Lord Jesus Christ. I thank God for you and for allowing Him to continue to use you in the body of Christ." (Oklahoma)

What Does God Say?

- "Your book *What Does God Say?* is one of the greatest books I have ever read. You tell the truth and back it up with Scripture. I started crime very young. I have spent a large portion of my life behind bars. I have so much to be ashamed of and things that I am very sorry for. I have almost wasted my life. I say almost because this book caused me to realize that God loves even me no matter what I have done. In your book I read that there is no condemnation in Christ Jesus. Do you have any idea what it means to feel no condemnation when society says to lock me up because I am guilty? My sins and all the crimes I have committed have been washed away. I cannot explain how it feels to know that someone is really proud of me. That someone is Jesus. I am taking this book home with me. Even though I don't have much education, I can understand it very well. I now know that I am saved and I am forgiven. Thank you very much for writing this book." (Florida)

- "Several months ago, you sent me a copy of your book titled *What Does God Say?*. This book is amazing. First of all, I could understand it. My English is not great. I have been a Muslim all my life. I was taught as a child what I was supposed to believe. When I was searching for real truth, I met the Master and received Jesus Christ as my Savior. When I read your book, it filled so much of the void and loneliness that I was filled with. I will be sharing Jesus and *What Does God Say?* with my family and with other Muslims. Please pray for me as I may not be welcomed in my own home town for finding this wonderful Jesus." (Ghana)

- "Our ministry here in South Africa is flourishing. We thank God for the books from Jack and Judy Hartman. The book, *What Does God Say?*, is my daily manual. It addresses all issues of life. I read it every day and I love it. I am complete. This book has made our ministry more effective. I no longer have to struggle on what to preach or teach. I am now equipped with the correct material. This book is filled with the anointing and revelation of God. My fellow pastors here in South Africa are hungry for these books. We soon will be opening a branch in Pretoria and also in Botswana. I thank God for the Hartmans. I always pray for them." (South Africa)

Quiet Confidence in the Lord

- "As soon as I was diagnosed with prostate cancer, I began to meditate on the Scripture and your explanation of the Scripture in *Quiet Confidence in the Lord.* I carried this book with me everywhere for several weeks. The specialist at the Lahey Clinic in Boston told me I was the calmest person with this diagnosis that he had ever seen. During the pre-op and the surgery, a number of people commented on how calm I was. I experienced a lot of discomfort during the difficult first week at home after the surgery. I focused constantly on the Scripture in this wonderful book. I was remarkably calm. Thank you for writing this book that has helped me so much." (Massachusetts)

- "After I graduated from Bible school, I went outside of my country for mission work with my wife. After we were there for nine months, my wife died suddenly. My sorrow was great. I read your book titled *Quiet Confidence in the Lord*. This book spoke to my heart. All twenty-three chapters were written for me. God changed me through this book and comforted me and took away my sorrow. Through the blood of Jesus I entered God's rest. I can give a great recommendation for this book to anyone who is filled with sorrow and grief. I pray that many people will read this book and develop quiet confidence in the Lord as I did. Thank you so much for sending this book to me. May God bless you and your ministry." (Ethiopia)

- "*Quiet Confidence in the Lord* is with me at work each day. I have read and underlined passages that lift my heart and help me to understand something I've known all along and that is that I am not alone and that God cares very much that I'm in the midst of great adversity. I asked God to send me a comforter, someone who would put their arms around me and say, 'I understand and I care.' The answer to that prayer is in you and Judy. Thanks to *Quiet Confidence of the Lord* I am, for the first time in my life, learning to focus on God and not my problems. Thank you both for your ministry. Your books are a tremendous blessing to hurting people all over the world." (Washington, DC)

- "Your great book, *Receive Healing from the Lord*, has amazed me. This book has been my daily bread. I have followed all of God's instructions in your book. My children and my wife were healed from severe illness. I was sick myself just before an important crusade. I meditated on the Scripture in your book for the entire night. I was totally healed. The following day God did wonders as He healed many people. Since then, people have been coming to receive their healing at our home and church almost every day. Many healings are taking place at our services. This book is wonderful. I am abundantly blessed by it." (Zambia)

- "My husband and I served in the mission field in Swaziland, Africa, for three and a half years. Upon our arrival, Lamplight Ministries sent us four mailbags full of Jack and Judy's books. Because Swaziland is so laden with HIV/AIDS, we were able to use the book, *Receive Healing from the Lord,* with the people in Swaziland to see many people come to a saving knowledge of the Lord Jesus Christ and His perfect will regarding healing. We saw mothers with very sick children who themselves also were afflicted with AIDS respond to the many Scriptures that are part of the book, actually believing that it was meant for them. Had it not been for the use of this book and the other books you sent, we would not have had such success in teaching a Bible study about the truth in God's Word to these people. We gave out your books and told the people that the book was theirs to keep. We saw such joy and surprise on the faces of these impoverished people. We appreciate the ongoing generosity of Lamplight Ministries for 'such a time as this' in these days where there is so much need and want. We will forever be thankful that we can count on the Word of

God through the books written by Jack and Judy as effective tools in the transformation of people's lives." (Swaziland)

- "Thank you very much for sending me your book, *Receive Healing from the Lord*. After reading the first chapter I realized that this book could be the solution for my wife's failing health. We decided to read the book together every day. My wife was healed and restored after carefully following the scriptural principles that you explained. We are humbled by how we had struggled and panicked trying to find an answer. God gave us the solution in your book. We are so grateful to you. We love you and we are praying for you." (Zambia)

What Will Heaven Be Like?
- "On the very first page of your book on heaven I was spellbound. The material read so quickly and coherently that it was like having a conversation with a Christian friend. I could really feel the excitement as we talked about the throne of God and its radiance. Those who are curious about heaven will be so delighted and joyful when they read this book. I think the questions at the end of the book are a great idea. This book is a ready-made classroom treasure. I was deeply moved by the gentle loving approach and the manner this material was presented to me, the reader. I can hardly wait to read your other books. You have gained a new fan and admirer of your special way of presenting the kingdom of heaven and God's love for us." (Mississippi)
- "I came to China from Cambodia where I was a captain in the army. I was a Buddhist. Four weeks before I came to China, I had a dream where Jesus appeared to me. When I woke up the following morning, I looked for Christians to explain more about Jesus Christ to me. After I came to China, I met a Christian man who gave me the

book *What Will Heaven Be Like?*. This book answered many questions for me. My English is not very good, but this book is written in very simple English. I have found new life through this book. Please pray for me so that I can share Jesus with my parents and my Buddhist friends when I go back to Cambodia." (China)

- "I am the Youth Director of our church and I'm leading a group of high school students in a Bible study of your book on heaven. We all respect your opinions and have found your book to be an excellent springboard for discussion. It is thought-provoking and informative. This book has much substance and is well organized." (California)

Never, Never Give Up

- "I am a 68-year-old businessman. At my age I should be enjoying a life way past retirement. It is not so. In 1997 Thailand suffered a severe economic crunch and my business almost went down under. It took me many years to try to come back. Just as I thought I was climbing out of the black hole, another crisis hit two years ago. This time I am too old to fight, but I have no choice but to go on. I thought that God and I were very close. However, after the first crisis hit I sort of lost my faith along with my hope. After the second crisis hit, I thought that God had forsaken me. I all but lost my faith totally until one day a good friend gave me a book, *Never, Never Give Up*. At first I didn't want to read it. However, insisted by my friend, I did. I stayed up the whole night finishing the book. By morning I kneeled down and begged God to forgive me for my foolishness. I felt so ashamed for my behavior. I begged Him to accept me back. After I did that, I know that God has forgiven me. Now I am back to feeling close to Him again. I am so happy and grateful for this book. God is great!" (Thailand)

- "Thanks for being there when you are so much needed by all of us. After seven major operations I am beginning to walk again and help others which is the full purpose of my existence which Jesus Christ has set before me. Your book, *Never, Never Give Up*, stayed by my pillow along with my Bible while I was recuperating from these operations. When I re-read it, I was charged with peace and energy again. The pain diminishes and I can speak of God's infinite love and mercy to others who are facing similar trials. Thank you for writing this God-inspired book." (Florida)

- "Suicide has shown its face in my mind. I found myself falling deeper and deeper into the pit of hell. My life seemed so grim. I could not see where I could make a difference and was planning to believe that if I chose to leave this life it would not matter. When I received *Never, Never Give Up* I read the first three chapters that evening. When I arrived at page ninety, your verse changed my life. I want you to know that I have been delivered from this season of trial. I rededicated my life to the Lord and feel wonderful. Thank you so much for your work. Through our Lord you have saved my life. Thank you for my life back." (Texas)

Overcoming Fear

- "Thank you for sending your books to the Philippines. I was very blessed to read *Overcoming Fear*. This book explained the sources of fear and what I should do to overcome fear. It is really a blessing to know all of this information that helped me to overcome the fear I have felt all these years. I have cherished every chapter in the book. It has become food for my soul. Thank you so much for explaining all of this so well. I have learned that I should never be afraid of anyone because I can be absolutely certain that God lives in my heart. This is great assurance because I know that God is greater than anything I will ever face in this life. This book has been a great blessing in my life. God bless you both." (the Philippines)

- "I want to thank you immediately for your new book, *Overcoming Fear.* I have read every one of your books and given copies to many people, but I want to tell you that I believe this is your best book ever. I can hardly put it down. The day I received it I stayed up late, even though I was very tired, to read the first four chapters. The next morning I read two more chapters before going to work. This book is very inspiring. It gives me great peace. God's peace is so great that I cannot describe it. I have almost finished reading this book. When I am done, I will immediately read it again. Enclosed is a check for ten copies of this book plus a contribution to Lamplight Ministries. Thank you, Jack and Judy, for writing this wonderful book." (Massachusetts)

- "I want to thank you for publishing the book *Overcoming Fear.* I am reading mine for the second time. I cannot tell you how comforting it is. The way you have put information along with the right Bible verses is so truly helpful. As world conditions worsen, I can tell you that this book will be a constant companion alongside my Bible. I am so grateful for you both. Keep up the good work. You are making a big difference in peoples' lives. You have in mine." (Minnesota)

Victory Over Adversity

- "I am a pure and proud Dutchman married to a Tanzanian woman. I have had a lot of problems staying with an African wife in Europe. I love my wife so much, but the environment for my wife was not good enough in terms of getting a job. This affected us very much to the extent that I was even planning to relocate to Tanzania for the sake of my wife and children's future. Thank God that an angel was sent to me by the name of Jim who gave me a book, *Victory over Adversity*. This book is amazing and great. It contains the answers to my problems and is a great encouragement to me. As a Dutchman I find it very interesting to read a book with simple English. Putting the facts of this book into practice has changed my life greatly. I have found a new job. My wife has found a good job. The thoughts of relocating to Tanzania have faded. My faith has increased and my commitment to God has grown. I pray that God will bless the writers of this book and also the man who gave me this book. My wife and I are always reading this book. It is our source of strength." (Holland)

- "I praise God for His living Word. Thank you for the books that you have sent to China. You cannot imagine what *Victory over Adversity* did in my life as a young believer. Not only is the language clear and accessible, but the content is very rewarding. I learned a lot from this book. I now meditate day and night on the Word of God. I am in the presence of God often. I am confident that I can overcome any adversity in the precious name of Jesus Christ. May God bless you and fill you with His infinite grace, Mr. Jack and his wife." (China)

- "I am a 22-year-old college student in Thailand. My family is half Christian. My mother is a Christian whereas my father is a Buddhist. I am the eldest daughter of my parents with one younger brother and sister. All three of us have been baptized as Christians since birth. Frankly, I have never had much faith in God and always have had problems with both of my parents. I think that they don't understand me. They think I don't listen to them. Last month my mother was given a book, *Victory over Adversity,* by her friend. Out of curiosity I took the book and read it before she did. I could not put it down. For the first time I felt that God is real and is close to me. I cried and cried and felt sorry for my past behavior toward God and my parents. I went to my mother and apologized, to her great surprise. Now I go to church with her every Sunday. I am very thankful to my mother's friend who gave her this book and also to the writers of this book who have changed my life and brought me to God which my mother could not do. Thank you both!" (Thailand)

Exchange Your Worries for God's Perfect Peace

- "*Exchange Your Worries for God's Perfect Peace* is a masterpiece. I am reading this book to the people here in the Philippines. I saw tears flowing down their faces as I read them parts of this book. I must get this book translated into their language. I am reading this book for the second time. After 30 years in the ministry I have finally learned how to turn my worries over to God. I have learned more from this book in the last few months than I have ever learned in my life. I will not allow my copy of this book to leave my presence. I thank God for you." (the Philippines)

- "I just want to tell you how much I appreciate you and your excellent book, *Exchange Your Worries for God's Perfect Peace*. I have read all of your books several times each. I continually go back to refer to the notes I have made in your books. I have done this for close to 15 years and pages are falling out of your books. I read the Bible daily. Your books are a close second to the Bible. I have never found another Christian author who teaches me more about God's Word and speaks directly to my heart as your writings do. Thank you for helping me appreciate and respect the Word of God." (Wisconsin)

- "I was in despair struggling with my life and ministry. *Exchange Your Worries for God's Perfect Peace* has strengthened me and encouraged my heart. My country is often threatened by disasters. Your book and the Scripture in it has helped me to focus on God, no matter what circumstances I have experienced and will face in the future. The language in the book is very clear and easy to understand for someone like me who uses English as a second language. I have been blessed by reading this book. My faith in Jesus has increased. Thank you for sending this book to me. I thank God that I know you. You are a blessing." (Indonesia)

God's Joy Regardless of Circumstances

- "*God's Joy Regardless of Circumstances* came to me right on time. Being in prison for 20 years for a crime I didn't commit and then having to deal with severe family problems is not a morsel that is easy to swallow. My oldest daughter was pregnant and we were looking forward to having my first grandson born. We were very pained to learn that my daughter had to lose her baby. In the midst of dealing with this problem, you sent me a free copy of *God's Joy Regardless of Circumstances*. When I avidly started to read this book, my daughter underwent surgery, lost her baby and faced uncertainty and despair. *God's Joy Regardless of Circumstances* pulled us through. Thank you also for sending a free copy of this book to my daughter. May God continue blessing Lamplight Ministries." (Florida)

- "Many thanks for sending me *God's Joy Regardless of Circumstances*. This book has been a real stream in the desert that I have been able to drink from. I have been blessed tremendously by this book. My life has not been the same since I started reading it. I have used this book to help many people on my radio programme every Sunday. Many people have given their lives to Christ because of these messages." (Zambia)

- "Only this year I faced a lot of challenges. As a result I became bitter at heart. The wonderful Scripture verses in *God's Joy Regardless of Circumstances* took away my bitterness. I am happy now. This book has instructed me how to handle any situation with God's joy. I now can see God's solution to my life challenges by the presence of God's joy inside me. Your God-given insight has given new meaning to my spiritual life. Thank you for the encouragement through your writings." (Lome-Togo West Africa)

God's Wisdom Is Available to You

- "I did not sleep last night after reading your book *God's Wisdom is Available to You.* Thank you for your wonderful work. Because of persecution against my ministry, I spent a considerable amount of time in the hospital because of depression. I am now well and healthy in Jesus' name. Thank you for your help. I will be teaching members of my church from key text in your book. Please be my mentor, teacher and counselor." (Ghana)
- "I thank God each and every day for Jack and Judy Hartman. When I started reading your book on wisdom, everything was going wrong in my life. This book revived my spirit and my faith in God. It has changed my life. The Bible used to be like Greek to me. Now I can read it and understand it. I can't put this book down because I know I need to absorb it. I'm going through it for a second time. This book is one of the best things that has ever happened to me. I thank you both and I thank God." (Florida)
- "You did a fantastic job on this book. It is an encyclopedia on God's wisdom. The writing style is just great. Many books don't bring the reader through the subject the way this book does. I'm very impressed with that. You have made it a real joy for me to study and re-digest Scripture. This book has been very good for me." (North Carolina)

A Close and Intimate Relationship with God

- "Your book, *A Close and Intimate Relationship with God,* is tremendous. I thought that I had a close relationship with God, but this book really opened my eyes. I now can see many things that I still need to do to be even closer to God. I couldn't put this book down. When I had to stop reading, I couldn't wait to get back to it the next day. Every chapter is filled with Scripture that is very helpful to me. I will be making many changes in my life as a result of reading this awesome book. Thank you and God bless you." (New Hampshire)

- "Thank you for giving me a copy of your book *A Close and Intimate Relationship with God.* This book is written so clearly that all instructions are to the point. My life has been greatly changed and refreshed. The presence of God has become very strong in my life. I am at peace trusting my God to meet every need. My mind is totally on God. I can clearly hear His voice. I am receiving guidance and direction from Him as a result of this book. I cannot afford to spend a day without reading this book. I carry it with me wherever I go." (Zambia)

- "Thank you for your book titled *A Close and Intimate Relationship with God.* This inspiring book helped me to draw closer to our heavenly Father. In Chapter 25 you said that Paul and Silas were praising God in prison. I was having a challenging day when I read this chapter. God spoke through your book to praise Him no matter what circumstances I faced. Thank you for that inspiration. The information on dying to self in the last chapter where Paul said that he dies daily really encouraged me. I am learning to do much better putting God first, others second and myself last. Thank you at Lamplight Ministries for the thousands of people around the world that you are supporting. May the dear Lord bless you abundantly." (China)

Unshakable Faith in Almighty God

- "I thank God for the book *Unshakable Faith in Almighty God*. Because I am not indigenous Chinese, it is not easy to fellowship with the local Chinese. When I got this book I was able to see a way in the wilderness. It became my guide and light every day. When I was just about to give up Christianity, God at the right time provided this book to me. The truths and clear instruction in this book are direct from the throne of God. I am determined to move on with God come what may. I praise God that is He able to raise people we have never seen like Jack and Judy Hartman to speak into our lives through their publications. God bless the Hartman family. One day when Christ comes it will be exciting for them to see how they have influenced the world for God in Jesus' name. I am so grateful for these free books that cost a lot of money in publishing, printing and postage." (China)

- "I have been pastoring in Belgium for the past 15 years. In the past our church was flourishing and doing very well until late last year when my praise and worship leader decided to break away and form another church. This was a very big blow to us as a church. Most of our strong and committed members left the church with some of the church instruments. My wife almost gave up. She was discouraged. This also affected our finances. Pastor Jim gave me a book titled *Unshakable Faith in Almighty God*. Before I read this book my faith was shaken and I almost gave up. This book took me step by step to show me how to make my faith grow. You cannot read this book and remain the same. I have been using the book to preach to the few members that remain with us. In the past four months we have experienced revival. The anointing is so strong and the members have been strengthened so much through the preaching from this book. We are determined to not give up. God bless the Hartmans for being a blessing to us in Europe." (Belgium)

- "*Unshakable Faith in Almighty God* has amazed me. The language is so simple and very clear to understand. This book is powerful and life-changing. I will always hang on to this book. Brother Hartman, God's favour and wisdom are so great on your life. I believe this book is written on very heavy anointing from God. Your reward in heaven will be so great. All those who have sown seeds in your ministry should rejoice. When I wake up, I read this book. Before going to bed, I read it. I will continue to go through it again and again. Your ministry is a big blessing to me. You are always in our prayers." (Zambia)

How to Study the Bible

- "Your book, *How to Study the Bible*, is a gem. Since I became a Christian 41 years ago, I have studied the Bible using a variety of methods. Your method is simple and straightforward. It involves hard work, but the rewards are real. I have read several of your books and this book is the one I would highly recommend to any Christian because this book is the foundation. God bless you, brother." (England)
- "My wife and I are utilizing the Bible study method that you explained in *How to Study the Bible*. We are really growing spiritually as a result. Our old methods of study were not nearly as fruitful. Thank you for writing about your method." (Idaho)
- "I have read almost all of your books and they are outstanding. The one that blessed me the most was *How to Study the Bible*. The study part was excellent, but the meditation chapters were very, very beneficial. I am indebted to you for sharing these. I purchased 30 copies

to give to friends. Every earnest student of God's Word needs a copy." (Tennessee)

Increased Energy and Vitality

- "It is so great to meet Christians on the same wave length. In your book *Increased Energy and Vitality*, you are writing almost word for word in some cases what I have been saying to patients for almost 30 years." (Ohio)
- "Last year I obtained a copy of your book *Increased Energy and Vitality.* My wife and I have read and have in fact changed our ways of eating and drinking and exercising because of your influence. We thoroughly appreciate this God-centered message that is so well presented. I have enclosed an order for more of these books. We know many people we wish to help. This is the first step in spreading the news you have so generously put together. Thank you for your efforts. May God continue your leadership in writing, speaking and guidance." (Illinois)
- "I have benefited tremendously from reading and personally applying the principles learned from your book *Increased Energy and Vitality.* By applying your methods, I have gained additional energy especially during my low periods from 2:00 p.m. to 4:00 p.m. I highly recommend your book to others. Keep up the good work." (Florida)

100 Years from Today

- "*100 Years From Today* told me that going to church and doing good deeds won't get me to heaven. I believe in Jesus Christ. I believe He died for our sins and that He forgives us for what we did wrong. Heaven is where I belong. I am born again. I have a new life. This book has changed my life." (Florida)
- "I am writing to express my deep and profound appreciation for your book *100 Years from Today*. I

recently began attending a Bible-based church where I found a copy of this book in their lending library. I read the book in one sitting, reading the words aloud to myself. Your book explained details from the Bible that I had not learned before. I thank you for taking the time and effort to write this book. My written words can never fully express how grateful I am to you. By my actions, a changed life and a deep sense of peace, I hope to bear fruit by helping others." (Massachusetts)

- "I find it hard to put *100 Years from Today* down. I read the whole book in a day and a half. I never knew how much pain and suffering Jesus went through to pay for my sins. I learned how much He loves us." (Florida)

Nuggets of Faith

- "Your books, tapes and meditation cards are really a blessing to me. They came at just the right time. I am preparing sermons on faith from *Nuggets of Faith*. I want the congregation to be constantly learning God's Word in order to have much more faith. I also have been encouraged personally through that book. It is awesome. Thank you for your powerful and inspiring publications." (Zambia)

- "We give *Nuggets of Faith* to people who are hospitalized, for birthdays, to saved and unsaved. Everyone who has received one tells us 'It's the best little book I've ever read. It's so clear and easy to understand.'" (Indiana)

- "I work as a store manager. Today I was told that I was no longer needed. Praise Jesus that only two months prior to this date I had accepted the Lord Jesus as my personal Lord and Savior. I have faith that the Lord was working to bring me to a new direction. I am writing to thank you for your excellent book *Nuggets of Faith*. The moment I arrived home after having been dismissed, I received this book in the mail. I completed this short but awesome book in a little over two hours. It has helped my faith to grow stronger and I know that I will begin a great new journey tomorrow. God bless you." (New York)

Comments on our Scripture Meditation Cards

- "My back was hurting so badly that I couldn't get comfortable. I was miserable whether I sat or stood or laid down. I didn't know what to do. Suddenly I thought of the Scripture cards on healing that my husband had purchased. I decided to meditate on the Scripture in these cards. I was only on the second card when, all of a sudden, I felt heat go from my neck down through my body. The Lord had healed me. I never knew it could happen so fast. The pain has not come back." (Idaho)
- "My wife and I use your Scripture cards every day when we pray. I read the card for that day in English and then my wife repeats it in Norwegian. We then pray based upon the Scripture reference on that day's card. These cards have been very beneficial to us. We would like to see the Scripture cards published in the Norwegian language." (Norway)
- "Your Scripture cards have been very helpful to my wife and myself. We have taped them to the walls in our home and we meditate on them constantly. I also take four or five cards with me every day when I go to work. I meditate on them while I drive. The Scripture on these cards is a constant source of encouragement to us. We ask for permission to translate *Trust God for Your Finances*. This

book is badly needed by the people in Turkey." (This permission was granted.) (Turkey)

- "My mom is 95 years old. She was in the Bergen-Belsen Concentration Camp in Germany from 1943 to 1945. She has always had a lot of worry and fear. My mother was helped greatly in overcoming this problem by your Scripture cards titled *Freedom from Worry and Fear*. She was helped so much that she asked me to order another set to give to a friend." (California)

- "I am overwhelmed about the revelations in your Scripture Meditation Cards. These Scripture cards have helped me so much that I cannot write enough on this sheet of paper. We have gone through a five-day programme in our church using the Scripture cards. My faith has increased tremendously. I no longer am submitting to my own will and desires, but I am now submitting to the will of God and it is so fantastic. God bless you, Jack and Judy Hartman." (Ghana)

- "I am very enthusiastic about your Scripture cards and your tape titled *Receive Healing from the Lord*. I love your tape. The clarity of your voice and your sincerity and compassion will encourage sick people. They can listen to this tape throughout the day, before they go to sleep at night, while they are driving to the doctor's office, in the hospital, etc. The tape is filled with Scripture and many good comments on Scripture. This cassette tape and your Scripture cards on healing are powerful tools that will help many sick people." (Tennessee) (NOTE: The ten cassette tapes for our Scripture Meditation Cards are available on 60 minute CDs as well.)

- "I meditate constantly on the healing cards and listen to your tape on healing over and over. Your voice is so soothing. You are a wonderful teacher. My faith is increasing constantly." (New Hampshire).

- "I thank God for you. I carry your Scripture Meditation Cards in my purse. The Scriptures you have chosen are all powerful. What a blessing to be able to meditate on the Word of God at any time, anywhere. Thank you for your hard work. The Scripture cards are a blessing to me." (Canada)

We offer you a substantial quantity discount

From the beginning of our ministry we have been led of the Lord to offer the same quantity discount to individuals that we offer to Christian bookstores. Each individual has a sphere of influence with a specific group of people. We believe that you know many people who need to learn the scriptural contents of our publications.

The Word of God encourages us to give freely to others. We encourage you to give selected copies of these publications to people you know who need help in the specific areas that are covered by our publications. See our order form for specific information on the quantity discounts that we make available to you so that you can share our books, Scripture Meditation Cards and CDs with others.

A request to our readers

If this book has helped you, we would like to receive your comments so that we can share them with others. Your comments can encourage other people to study our publications to learn from the scriptural contents of these publications.

When we receive a letter containing comments on any of our books, cassette tapes or Scripture Meditation Cards, we prayerfully take out excerpts from these letters. These selected excerpts are included in our newsletters and occasionally in our advertising and promotional materials.

If any of our publications have been a blessing to you, please share your comments with us so that we can share them with others. Tell us in your own words what a specific publication has meant to you and why you would recommend it to others. Please give as much specific information as possible. We prefer three or four paragraphs so that we can condense this into one paragraph.

Thank you for taking a few minutes of your time to encourage other people to learn from the scripture references in our publications.

ORDER FORM FOR BOOKS

Book Title	Quantity	Total
What Does God Say? ($18)	_____ x $18 =	_____
God's Plan for Your Life ($14)	_____ x $18 =	_____
You Can Hear the Voice of God ($14)	_____ x $14 =	_____
Effective Prayer ($14)	_____ x $14 =	_____
God's Instructions for Growing Older ($14)	_____ x $14 =	_____
A Close and Intimate Relationship with God ($14)	_____ x $14 =	_____
God's Joy Regardless of Circumstances ($14)	_____ x $14 =	_____
Victory Over Adversity ($14)	_____ x $14 =	_____
Receive Healing from the Lord ($14)	_____ x $14 =	_____
Unshakable Faith in Almighty God ($14)	_____ x $14 =	_____
Exchange Your Worries for God's Perfect Peace ($14)	_____ x $14 =	_____
God's Wisdom is Available to You ($14)	_____ x $14 =	_____
Overcoming Fear ($14)	_____ x $14 =	_____
Trust God For Your Finances ($10)	_____ x $10 =	_____
What Will Heaven Be Like? ($10)	_____ x $10 =	_____
Quiet Confidence in the Lord ($10)	_____ x $10 =	_____
Never, Never Give Up ($10)	_____ x $10 =	_____
Increased Energy and Vitality ($10)	_____ x $10 =	_____
How to Study the Bible ($7)	_____ x $7 =	_____
Nuggets of Faith ($7)	_____ x $7 =	_____
100 Years From Today ($7)	_____ x $7 =	_____

Price of books _____

Minus 40% discount for 5-9 books _____

Minus 50% discount for 10 or more books _____

Net price of order _____

Add 15% **before discount** for shipping and handling _____

Florida residents only, add 7% sales tax _____

Tax deductible contribution to Lamplight Ministries, Inc. _____

Enclosed check or money order (do not send cash) _____

(Foreign orders must be submitted in U.S. dollars.)

Please make check payable to **Lamplight Ministries, Inc**. and mail to:
PO Box 1307, Dunedin, FL 34697

MC_____   Visa_____   AmEx_____   Disc._____   Card # _____

Exp Date _____   Signature _____

Name _____

Address _____

City _____

State or Province _____   Zip or Postal Code _____

Email _____   Website: _____

ORDER FORM FOR BOOKS

Book Title	Quantity	Total
What Does God Say? ($18)	_____ x $18 =	_____
God's Plan for Your Life ($14)	_____ x $18 =	_____
You Can Hear the Voice of God ($14)	_____ x $14 =	_____
Effective Prayer ($14)	_____ x $14 =	_____
God's Instructions for Growing Older ($14)	_____ x $14 =	_____
A Close and Intimate Relationship with God ($14)	_____ x $14 =	_____
God's Joy Regardless of Circumstances ($14)	_____ x $14 =	_____
Victory Over Adversity ($14)	_____ x $14 =	_____
Receive Healing from the Lord ($14)	_____ x $14 =	_____
Unshakable Faith in Almighty God ($14)	_____ x $14 =	_____
Exchange Your Worries for God's Perfect Peace ($14)	_____ x $14 =	_____
God's Wisdom is Available to You ($14)	_____ x $14 =	_____
Overcoming Fear ($14)	_____ x $14 =	_____
Trust God For Your Finances ($10)	_____ x $10 =	_____
What Will Heaven Be Like? ($10)	_____ x $10 =	_____
Quiet Confidence in the Lord ($10)	_____ x $10 =	_____
Never, Never Give Up ($10)	_____ x $10 =	_____
Increased Energy and Vitality ($10)	_____ x $10 =	_____
How to Study the Bible ($7)	_____ x $7 =	_____
Nuggets of Faith ($7)	_____ x $7 =	_____
100 Years From Today ($7)	_____ x $7 =	_____

Price of books _____

Minus 40% discount for 5-9 books _____

Minus 50% discount for 10 or more books _____

Net price of order _____

Add 15% **before discount** for shipping and handling _____

Florida residents only, add 7% sales tax _____

Tax deductible contribution to Lamplight Ministries, Inc. _____

Enclosed check or money order (do not send cash) _____

(Foreign orders must be submitted in U.S. dollars.)

Please make check payable to **Lamplight Ministries, Inc**. and mail to:
PO Box 1307, Dunedin, FL 34697

MC_____ Visa_____ AmEx_____ Disc._____ Card # _____

Exp Date _____ Signature _____

Name _____

Address _____

City _____

State or Province _____ Zip or Postal Code _____

Email _____ Website: _____

ORDER FORM FOR SCRIPTURE MEDITATION CARDS AND CDs

SCRIPTURE MEDITATION CARDS	QUANTITY	PRICE
Find God's Will for Your Life ($5)		
Financial Instructions from God ($5)		
Freedom from Worry and Fear ($5)		
A Closer Relationship with the Lord ($5)		
Our Father's Wonderful Love ($5)		
Receive Healing from the Lord ($5)		
Receive God's Blessing in Adversity ($5)		
Enjoy God's Wonderful Peace ($5)		
God is Always with You ($5)		
Continually Increasing Faith in God ($5)		

CDs	QUANTITY	PRICE
Find God's Will for Your Life ($10)		
Financial Instructions from God ($10)		
Freedom from Worry and Fear ($10)		
A Closer Relationship with the Lord ($10)		
Our Father's Wonderful Love ($10)		
Receive Healing from the Lord ($10)		
Receive God's Blessing in Adversity ($10)		
Enjoy God's Wonderful Peace ($10)		
God is Always with You ($10)		
Continually Increasing Faith in God ($10)		

TOTAL PRICE

Minus 40% discount for 5-9 Scripture Cards and CDs

Minus 50% discount for 10 or more Scripture Cards and CDs

Net price of order

Add 15% **before discount** for shipping and handling

Florida residents only, add 7% sales tax

Tax deductible contribution to Lamplight Ministries, Inc.

Enclosed check or money order (do not send cash)

(Foreign orders must be submitted in U.S. dollars.)

Please make check payable to **Lamplight Ministries, Inc**. and mail to:
PO Box 1307, Dunedin, FL 34697

MC_____ Visa_____ AmEx_____ Disc._____ Card # _____

Exp Date _____ Signature _____

Name _____

Address _____

City _____

State or Province _____ Zip or Postal Code _____

Email _____ Website: _____

ORDER FORM FOR SCRIPTURE MEDITATION CARDS AND CDs

SCRIPTURE MEDITATION CARDS	QUANTITY	PRICE
Find God's Will for Your Life ($5)	_____	_____
Financial Instructions from God ($5)	_____	_____
Freedom from Worry and Fear ($5)	_____	_____
A Closer Relationship with the Lord ($5)	_____	_____
Our Father's Wonderful Love ($5)	_____	_____
Receive Healing from the Lord ($5)	_____	_____
Receive God's Blessing in Adversity ($5)	_____	_____
Enjoy God's Wonderful Peace ($5)	_____	_____
God is Always with You ($5)	_____	_____
Continually Increasing Faith in God ($5)	_____	_____

CDs	QUANTITY	PRICE
Find God's Will for Your Life ($10)	_____	_____
Financial Instructions from God ($10)	_____	_____
Freedom from Worry and Fear ($10)	_____	_____
A Closer Relationship with the Lord ($10)	_____	_____
Our Father's Wonderful Love ($10)	_____	_____
Receive Healing from the Lord ($10)	_____	_____
Receive God's Blessing in Adversity ($10)	_____	_____
Enjoy God's Wonderful Peace ($10)	_____	_____
God is Always with You ($10)	_____	_____
Continually Increasing Faith in God ($10)	_____	_____

TOTAL PRICE _____

Minus 40% discount for 5-9 Scripture Cards and CDs _____
Minus 50% discount for 10 or more Scripture Cards and CDs _____
Net price of order _____
Add 15% **before discount** for shipping and handling _____
Florida residents only, add 7% sales tax _____
Tax deductible contribution to Lamplight Ministries, Inc. _____
Enclosed check or money order (do not send cash) _____
(Foreign orders must be submitted in U.S. dollars.)

Please make check payable to **Lamplight Ministries, Inc**. and mail to:
PO Box 1307, Dunedin, FL 34697

MC_____ Visa_____ AmEx_____ Disc._____ Card # _____

Exp Date _____ Signature _____

Name _____

Address _____

City _____

State or Province _____ Zip or Postal Code _____

Email _____ Website: _____